"NO-Yelli Parenting Toolbox

Peaceful Parenting Simplified:

Effective Strategies for Calm Communication, Managing Kids' Tantrums, and Strengthening Family Connections

Carrie Khang

Before you begin, go grab a **FREE GIFT!**

Get your Free Printables

Scan me

CONTENTS

Part 4: Final Thoughts

INTRODUCTION

I f you're reading this book, chances are you've experienced the sweet and bitter sides of parenting.

Welcome to the whirlwind adventure of parenting, a journey where each day brings its own blend of laughter and tears, triumphs and trials. This isn't just another parenting book; it's a real, raw, and relatable guide through the labyrinth of raising children.

Picture this: one moment, your heart swells with pride as your little one whispers "I love you," their tiny fingers wrapped around yours. These are the magical, Instagram-worthy moments every parent cherishes. But then, as quickly as they come, these moments are replaced by the chaotic, hair-pulling episodes of midnight wails or public meltdowns. Your parenting journey also includes navigating tantrums over mismatched socks when you're trying to get your child to school on time, or choices of cereal in a supermarket aisle.

As a parenting coach, I've seen everything from those tender, heartwarming moments to the full-on, stressful ones. My own parenting journey has had its share of colorful tales too, like a peaceful

Saturday morning breakfast that suddenly turned into a grocery store run, all because of a little disagreement over a toy.

In this book, we're going to get real about parenting. It's not just about making sure the kids are fed and safe. It's about guiding them to grow up as caring, confident people. And truth be told, there's no magic handbook for that. Every kid is different, and so are you. But here's the bright side: you're not in this alone. With the right approach, even the tricky parts of parenting can become smoother and more manageable.

I've been there – starting out as a parent, feeling a bit out of control, then gradually becoming a calmer, more understanding force in my child's life. But it didn't happen overnight. It was all about recognizing my feelings, figuring out what was really getting under my skin, and seeing each challenge as a chance to grow closer to my child and stronger as a parent.

Think of this book as your friendly guide through the wilds of parenting. Each chapter is a bite-sized nugget of wisdom, just right for those rare, quiet moments that parents treasure. Whether you're soothing your toddler's tears or trying to really get through to your teen, you'll find down-to-earth tips and real talk within these pages.

We'll explore everything from figuring out what ticks you off to mastering the "No-Yelling Formula." We'll dive into topics that'll give you the know-how to face parenting head-on, with confidence and calm. Remember, parenting is beautifully imperfect. It's messy, it's hectic, but it's also filled with incredible love and lessons.

No matter where you're at in your parenting journey, this book is packed with insights for every part. Get ready to tackle each day with patience, a splash of humor, and heaps of love. Flip the page and embark on this exciting journey with me. Let's reshape parenting, one heartfelt, challenging, unforgettable day at a time.

PART 1

ANGER AND PARENTS

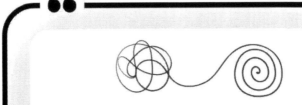

"ANGER IS OFTEN
MORE HURTFUL THAN
THE INJURY THAT
CAUSED IT."

@NOYELLINGPARENTINGTOOLBOX

C H A P T E R 1

PARENT ANGER

"You're driving me up the wall!"

We've all had those ugly moments when we feel like we'll blow a fuse, or we're ready to call it quits because our child's excesses hit an all-time high. Perhaps your child turns bedtime into a battlefield, there's a standoff over veggies, or they just refuse to listen to a word you say no matter how loudly you scream.

I've had moments that felt like I was close to having a meltdown myself. I've even worried I'd become a permanent fixture at the school principal's office because my child wouldn't stop talking back. Most parents have felt like failures at some point or another.

Parenting, as heartwarming as it can be, is also a rollercoaster of emotions — joy, love, laughter, irritation, frustration, and yes, even anger. Surprised? Don't be. Even the calmest among us aren't immune to the occasional eruption of emotions.

We're strapped in for that rollercoaster ride because it's unpredictable and thrilling, contains heart-pounding twists and turns, and sometimes makes us want to scream our lungs out. It's up to us to arm ourselves with helpful tools with which to ride safely.

This first chapter will dive into the roots of parent anger and common anger reactions. You know, those all-too-common scenarios that push our buttons and sometimes get the best of us? We'll discuss them here, so stay with me.

Roots of Parent Anger

Let's be real, parenting highs and lows can push us to the brink of anger. But it's not just about *being* mad; it's about what's brewing underneath that causes you to boil over. Understanding where your anger comes from is like finding the missing piece of a puzzle.

First, let's talk about **stress**. You've got bills to pay, work deadlines, and a mountain of laundry staring you down. Add a little one throwing a tantrum into that mix, and stress can turn into anger faster than a spilled cup of juice.

Let's not overlook **daily annoyances**. The toys scattered everywhere, the endless questions, the picky eating. It can be a constant test of your patience.

Next, there are **unmet expectations**. We all dream of picture-perfect parenting moments. But instead of sweet smiles, sometimes you end up dealing with backtalk and bedtime battles. That frustration can easily bubble up into an angry outburst.

Personal history plays a big part too. Think about how you were raised. Maybe you had super strict parents and now find yourself snapping when your kids don't follow the rules. Or perhaps you grew up in a home where yelling was the norm, and now you're repeating the cycle without even realizing it.

Don't forget about **emotional regulation**. It's like having a thermostat for your feelings. Sometimes, if it's set too high, the smallest thing can set you off. And if you're running on empty, with no "me time" in sight, that thermostat can go haywire.

Lack of sleep can be a major cause of a short fuse with your children. Ever tried to be the world's best parent on four hours of sleep? Everything's more irritating, and patience quickly wears thin.

Now, think about **communication** (or the lack of it). Maybe you're not on the same parenting page as your partner, or you feel like your kids just don't listen. You may feel like you're talking to a brick wall in both cases, and that can really crank up the frustration.

Lastly, there's the **feeling of losing your identity**. Sometimes, in the midst of parenting, you might feel like you've lost a bit of who you are, and that can lead to feelings of resentment or anger.

Understanding the roots of your anger is like putting on a new pair of glasses. Suddenly, things become clearer. It's not about being a bad parent; it's about being human. Once you understand where the anger is coming from, you can start working on cool-down strategies, finding that much-needed "me time," and turning those tough moments into opportunities for growth. So, let's take a deep breath, step back, and tackle this anger thing together.

There are parenting support groups and resources available in your community or online that can provide additional guidance and a sense of belonging. Don't hesitate to seek out these valuable sources of support as you embark on your parenting journey. Sharing your experiences and listening to others in local or online support groups can be incredibly helpful. Asking for help is not embarrassing; it's a courageous step towards letting go of your anger and becoming the best parent you can be.

Common Anger Reactions

1. Yelling

Kids can make even the most patient parents want to pull out their hair and resort to yelling.

Picture dinner time with your 6-year-old, Jack, who is glaring at his untouched vegetables. Despite your repeated requests, he refuses to eat. Overwhelmed with frustration, you find yourself yelling, "How many times do I have to tell you?! Eat your vegetables now!" It's a classic case of how frustration can get the better of you and lead to yelling.

2. Immediate Punishment

I believe we've all had moments when our patience runs thin, and we are pushed to impose consequences immediately.

Imagine a scenario where Sarah, your little artist, uses the living room wall as her canvas. The sight of crayon marks on the fresh paint pushes you to an impulsive decision: "No watching TV for a week!" This scenario exemplifies how frustration can lead to immediate, and often harsh, punishment.

3. Dismissal or Ignoring

Sometimes, dismissal, or ignoring the problem can be the easiest way for parents to avoid a public meltdown.

You're in a grocery store with little Tom. He throws a tantrum over a toy you won't buy. As onlookers glance your way, you choose to ignore his outburst and continue your shopping, hoping his tantrum will subside. This approach is often used to avoid public embarrassment.

4. Assuming Negative Intentions

It's easy for parents to assume negative intentions from their children when frustration creeps in.

Let's say you're on an important phone call, and your child, Sophie, excitedly interrupts to show you her drawing. Frustrated, you mute the call and respond, "Can't you see I'm busy? Don't be rude!!" This reaction is based on the assumption that your child's motive for entering the room was to intentionally disrupt your call, when instead, it was simply to share her excitement over her drawing.

5. Enabling Behavior

Have you ever found yourself saying yes to your child's whims just to dodge a meltdown? Many parents will understand that temptation.

At the grocery store, Alex zeroes in on his favorite treat. He pleads loudly, you feel the stares of other shoppers, and before you know it, the snack is in your cart. "Okay," you say, "but let's keep it cool for the rest of the trip." That's enabling behavior in a nutshell – caving to your child's wishes to sidestep a fuss or keep the peace.

Now, thinking about the five common reactions we've talked about. Which ones hit home for you? Personally, I've struggled with all of them, switching from one to the other. I've tried everything under the sun to calm my child, but ultimately it was a temporary fix; the tantrums always made a comeback.

Looking back, I see the flaw in my approach. It was all about the quick fix – no real lessons – and it was all based on how my child acted in the moment. As an inexperienced mom, I didn't know how to manage my own emotions effectively, so it was impossible to guide my son on how to manage and express his emotions in a healthy way.

Parent Anger Quiz

Take this quiz to get a clear picture of your parenting style in everyday situations. Honest answers will reveal if you're acing the parenting game, or if there's room for a little improvement. It's a quick, insightful way to see where you stand and how you can enhance your parenting journey. Just pick the responses that most sound like you, tally up your points, and discover your parenting anger management level.

1. Your child spills their drink on the floor.
   - "Not again! Why can't you be more careful?" while cleaning up with a frustrated sigh. (3 points)
   - "You need to clean this up now – and be more careful next time," in a firm tone. (4 points)
   - "Oops! No worries, these things happen. Let's clean it up together," with a smile. (1 point)
   - "Well, you made the mess. You clean it up," without offering to help. (2 points)

2. Your child is not ready on time for school.

- "Every morning it's the same story! Hurry up!" with noticeable irritation. (3 points)
- "You're late again. Next time, get up when I tell you to," in a stern voice. (4 points)
- "Looks like someone's running a bit late. Let's see how we can speed this up," calmly. (1 point)
- Muttering under your breath about being late but not saying anything directly. (2 points)

3. Your child is throwing a tantrum in a public place.

- "What's wrong, sweetheart? Can you tell me?" while kneeling to their level. (1 point)
- Trying to bribe them with a treat to stop the tantrum, feeling stressed. (3 points)
- Quickly steering them away from the scene to avoid further embarrassment. (2 points)
- "Stop that right now! Everyone is looking at us!" with a flushed face. (4 points)

4. Your child forgets to do their homework.

- "This is important – you can't keep forgetting your homework!" with worry in your voice. (3 points)
- "Let's sit down and see how we can remember next time. Do you need a planner?" helpfully. (1 point)
- "Again? You need to start taking this seriously!" visibly upset. (4 points)
- Rolling your eyes but deciding not to say anything about it. (2 points)

5. Your child won't eat their vegetables.

- "You're not leaving this table until you eat your veggies," with a stern look. (4 points)

- "How about dessert after a few bites of these veggies?" trying to negotiate. (3 points)
- "Vegetables are good for you. Let's talk about why they're important," in a gentle tone. (1 point)
- Feeling annoyed, but deciding not to make it a big issue this time. (2 points)

6. Your child talks back to you disrespectfully.
- "That's no way to talk to me. You need to show some respect," firmly. (3 points)
- "We need to talk about how we speak to each other. Let's find a better way," calmly. (1 point)
- Feeling hurt, but asking, "Is something bothering you?" to understand their behavior. (2 points)
- Snapping back with a sharp retort, caught up in the moment. (4 points)

7. Your child is playing loudly while you're on a call.
- "Can't you see I'm on the phone? Be quiet!" gesturing for them to lower the noise. (4 points)
- Pointing at the phone and mouthing, "Be quiet," feeling disrupted. (3 points)
- After the call, explaining why it's important to be quiet during phone calls. (1 point)
- Trying to ignore the noise and focusing on your call, feeling a bit frustrated. (2 points)

Scoring:
- 7-10 points: Excellent anger management! You handle parenting challenges with patience and understanding.
- 11-17 points: Moderate anger level. You manage well in some situations, but there are moments when anger gets the better of you.

- 18-24 points: Above average anger level. Exploring new strategies for stress and anger management could be beneficial.
- 25-28 points: High anger level. It may be helpful to seek resources or support for better managing reactions and fostering a positive family environment.

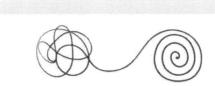

"DON'T LET YOUR ANGER
CONTROL YOU. DON'T LET
YOURSELF CONTROL YOUR
CHILD. LEAD BY CALM, LEAD
BY EXAMPLE."
– ANONYMOUS

@NOYELLINGPARENTINGTOOLBOX

C H A P T E R 2

KNOW YOUR TRIGGERS

Ever get really mad over something small and then later wonder why it bothered you so much? This chapter is all about that. Let's say your partner just had a shower and left the bathroom floor all wet, with water tracks leading to the bedroom. Most of us wouldn't be smiling about that. Instead, we'd probably be pretty annoyed, maybe even yell a bit. That feeling, that quick jump to annoyance or anger, is what we call a "trigger."

Do you know what sets off your triggers? Have you thought about why some little things your kids do can make you super mad, while your partner doesn't seem concerned in the least? Everyone's triggers are different. This chapter will help you figure out yours. We'll see why tiny things can make even the calmest person lose their cool and act in ways they wouldn't usually. We'll talk about what triggers are, why it's important to know about them, and then look at some examples. We want to help you understand those quick feelings of anger or annoyance and how to handle them better.

Most Common Triggers

Parenting triggers are those moments when our kids do or say something, and, suddenly, we're upset. Maybe we start yelling, crying, or even saying things we later regret. It's like one minute we're fine, and the next, we're really mad. This happens to the best of us.

So, what sets off these triggers? Let's break down some of the most common ones:

- **Kids Not Listening:** Imagine you're trying to explain something important to your child, but they're engrossed in their video game, headphones on, and totally ignoring you. Yep, that's a trigger.
- **Sibling Arguments**: Picture this: you're trying to work from home, and suddenly you hear your kids engaged in a loud argument over who gets control of the TV remote. Your stress levels shoot up. Welcome to trigger city.
- **Food Waste:** You've spent hours preparing a delicious homemade dinner, and your child takes one look at it and says, "I don't like this! I want something else." Many of us start thinking about how other less fortunate children could benefit from that food. Another classic trigger.

- **Children Talking Back:** It's tough when your usually sweet kid starts arguing with everything you say and questioning your authority. For example, you ask them to clean their room, and they respond with, "Why should I? It's my room." Definitely frustrating.
- **Whining:** Imagine your child repeatedly whining in a high-pitched tone about wanting a new toy while you're shopping. Those constant complaints about trivial matters can really test your patience.
- **Silliness:** Kids need to play and have fun, but sometimes their silliness can be overwhelming. Picture them running around the house, screaming and laughing, while you're trying to have a serious work call. That can get your blood pressure up
- **Tantrums and Big Emotions:** You're at the grocery store, and your child suddenly throws a full-blown tantrum because you won't buy them candy. Shoppers are staring, and you're trying to handle the situation. It can be overwhelming.
- **Lack of Privacy or Personal Space:** Ever feel like you can't get a moment alone? Imagine you're in the bathroom trying to have a moment of peace, and your child barges in with a million questions. Kids can invade your personal space, disrupting your privacy.

These are all common triggers for parents, which can set off an emotional outburst.

And it's interesting to see how triggers change as our kids grow up. For example, when my son was just a baby, his crying would make me feel panicked. My heart would beat fast, my hands would get sweaty, and I'd feel scared and a bit out of control. Now that he's a teenager, panic is more likely to set in if he's out late or participating in a risky activity.

It's good to remember that these feelings are normal. They're just part of being a parent. Everyone has different things that make them react strongly, and that's okay. The first step to handling these feelings better is to notice what makes us feel that way. Once we know, we can stay calm and help our kids in the best way, no matter how old they are.

Reflective Emotions

Just when you think you understand the rollercoaster of parenting, you're blindsided by your own emotions. It's one thing to identify the common triggers that set us off; it's another to confront the profound, reflective emotions they unearth. These aren't your garden-variety annoyances though. They're deep-seated, often surprising feelings that bubble up from our own life stories.

Have you ever wondered why you sometimes become irritated or angry in response to your child's minor actions? This phenomenon can often be attributed to "reflective emotions," which are our subconscious, automatic emotional reactions.

Reflective emotions can be thought of as emotions about emotions. They represent the parent's own feelings triggered by their child's emotions. These feelings may include sensations of empathy, discomfort, anger, sadness, embarrassment, or pity. For instance, you might experience anger as a reaction to being embarrassed in a certain situation, which is a classic example of reflective emotions.

Consider a scenario at the playground where, seeing your child hesitantly waiting for their turn on the swing but not speaking up, you might impulsively scold, "Just tell them it's your turn!" Later, you wonder why you were so angry at that moment. Perhaps it's because you were similarly scolded in your own childhood and, seeing your child's hesitancy and silence triggers those old feelings, resulting in anger.

Why is it important to read and understand your reflective emotions as a parent? Because to better understand and appropriately respond to our child's inner world, it can be beneficial to occasionally reflect on our own inner world.

When facing any issue involving our child, being aware of our own reflective emotions allows us to filter them out and thus focus on the child's feelings, rather than our own. By truly seeing the child as they are, we can respond to challenging situations with flexibility and wisdom.

Let's briefly examine our inner reflective emotions. Try filling in the ( ) with various emotions such as anger, fear, sadness, joy, etc., to explore how it applies.

- Have you had experiences related to (sadness) in your childhood?
- How did your family express (joy)?
- What was your mother/father like when (angry)?
- How did your parents react when you were (sad)?
- What do you do when you are (fearful)?
- What makes you (angry)?

A great way to help your *child* understand reflective emotions is by flipping through your own childhood photo albums together. As you both peek into these snapshots of your past, share little stories about what was happening in each photo and how you felt back then. It's like giving your child a friendly tour of your younger days! Plus, it may help bring to your attention some incidents responsible for your own reflective emotions.

You can make it even more relatable by connecting your stories to their experiences. For instance, you might find a photo of yourself looking a bit shy at a school event. Share that story! Tell them how you wanted to speak up boldly in front of your friends but ended up feeling all jittery and tongue-tied, just like how they might feel sometimes. It's a fun and cozy way to show your child that their feelings are understood and shared, bridging the gap between your worlds with warmth and empathy.

Yelling or No Yelling

We've all been there – that moment when the volume of our voice escalates, and we find ourselves yelling at our children. Deep down, we know it's counterproductive. Yelling doesn't really lead to positive changes. If anything, it often makes the atmosphere more tense. It's like shouting at your partner – it doesn't magically resolve issues, right?

So then, why do we yell? Often, it's an automatic response, a knee-jerk reaction to misbehavior or a situation spiraling out of our control. Sometimes, it's because we don't know any other way. Maybe we weren't shown different methods, or perhaps in the heat of the moment, we default to what we've unconsciously learned from our own upbringing.

It's crucial to recognize that yelling is less about your child's actions and more about your emotional state. During those intense moments, negative thoughts might cloud your mind: "I'm failing as a parent," "I'm invisible," "Nobody listens to or appreciates me," "I'm not good enough." But these thoughts are likely echoes from the past, not reflections of the present.

But why does this happen? Triggers are like time machines that transport you back to your past. Even after many years, old emotional wounds from your past can be activated, reminding you of the hurt and beliefs you've carried into adulthood.

This makes different people react differently to the same situation. For instance, you might find yourself getting angrier or more upset than your spouse over your child's behavior. You might even question why your partner thinks such behavior acceptable, when it clearly isn't to you. These differences in perception are rooted in the distinct family values and parenting styles each of you experienced growing up. Recognizing these differences is important. It helps in understanding that there isn't a one-size-fits-all approach to parenting.

They Push Your Buttons

It's a well-known mantra of parenting: your child will push your buttons. It's not about them trying to upset you; it's just part of being a kid. They're learning about the world, testing limits, and seeing what happens. So, expect it to happen, and try not to take it too personally.

Just like a weather-savvy person grabs an umbrella expecting rain, you can be a wise parent by anticipating these testing times. Your little one isn't out to get you; they're just being a child, doing childlike things. They're bound to misbehave or test boundaries – it's all part of growing up.

Your job is to stay calm and show them where the boundary lines are drawn. When they cross those lines, it's up to you to gently but firmly guide them back. This isn't about getting mad. It's about teaching them what's okay and what's not.

Think of it this way: you're the calm captain steering the ship through the choppy waters of childhood. Your kid is exploring, sometimes going off course. It's your job to navigate them back on track, without losing your cool. Expect these moments, be ready for them, and handle them with a steady hand. That's what great parenting is all about.

PART 2

YOU DON'T NEED TO YELL

"THE SIGN OF GREAT
PARENTING IS NOT THE
CHILD'S BEHAVIOR. THE SIGN
OF TRULY GREAT PARENTING
IS THE PARENT'S BEHAVIOR."
– ANDY SMITHSON

@NOYELLINGPARENTINGTOOLBOX

C H A P T E R 3

CALM IN THE CHAOS

Picture this: you're in the kitchen, baking cookies and making memories with your child. Laughter fills the air, mixed with the sweet scent of cookies in the oven. Suddenly, in a whirl of excitement, your little one's hands fumble, and a whole bag of flour cascades to the floor. As you both stand amidst this unexpected snowfall, you're at a crossroads: do you let frustration take over, or do you share a smile and turn it into a playful lesson?

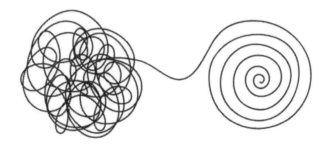

Welcome to "Calm in the Chaos." In this chapter, we embrace these flour-covered moments, recognizing them as perfect opportunities for teaching and bonding. It's not just about the mess, but about how we choose to respond to our little one's innocent mishaps. Together, let's sift through the flour and uncover the joy in these situations, transforming quick frustrations into moments of laughter and learning. This is where the real recipe for positive parenting begins – with a sprinkle of patience and a whole lot of love.

Respond, Don't React

It's incredibly easy to get swept up in the heat of a tantrum. The natural impulse is to react right away. But here's a secret: there's a better way to navigate this – and that's by responding, not reacting. *Reacting* often means acting on impulse, without thinking about the long-term impact. This can lead to saying or doing things in the heat of the moment that you might regret later. *Responding*, however, means taking a moment to breathe, assess the situation, and then address it in a calm, considered way. It's about understanding the heart of the issue and dealing with it in a way that doesn't throw more fuel on the emotional fire.

When you react, you're throwing *your* emotions back at your child's. They shout, you shout louder. It's like a match of emotional tennis. But responding is different. It's about creating a safe space for your child to express their big feelings, offering understanding and empathy without judgment. For instance, if your child is upset over something they perceive as unfair, instead of dismissing their feelings, you acknowledge their frustration and listen.

Let's look at some everyday scenarios to show the difference between reacting and responding:

- Reacting: "Stop that crying right now!"
- Responding: "You look really upset. How about a hug?

- Reacting: "What?! You spilled your juice again?"
- Responding: "Oops, spills happen. Let's clean it up together."

- Reacting: "How many times do I need to remind you to feed the dog?"
- Responding: "We keep forgetting about feeding the dog. Let's set up a reminder so we both remember."

- Reacting: "Another 'C' in math? What's happening?"
- Responding: "It looks like math is a bit tough right now. How can I help you improve?"

- Reacting: "Enough with the whining already."
- Responding: "I'm here to listen. Can you tell me what's bothering you using your normal voice?"

Just like how you automatically know that $1 + 1 = 2$, sometimes your reaction to your child's mistakes can be just as automatic – a quick yell without a second thought. But imagine you're on a diet, trying to shed a few pounds. You see a tempting slice of cake and you automatically want to eat it, but instead you pause, remember your goal, and choose a healthier snack. It's tough, sure, but you're making a conscious effort.

Now apply that to parenting. When your child spills a drink or breaks a toy, your first, automatic reaction might be to raise your voice. But what if you pause, take a breath, and respond calmly instead, just like choosing a healthy snack over cake? It's about retraining your automatic reactions, turning quick tempers into quick patience, one intentional choice at a time. Just like sticking to a diet, it's a daily effort, but one that gradually builds a healthier, happier home.

Are You Punishing?

We all acknowledge it's essential to be reasonable with our children, yet the distinction between punishment and consequences often becomes blurred. It's not uncommon for parents to confuse the two, sometimes resulting in unreasonable punishments mistakenly labeled as consequences.

The distinction is subtle yet significant. Punishing, whether it's through yelling, timeouts, or taking things away, can leave kids feeling pretty lousy. And the worst part is it doesn't really teach them what they need to learn.

Consequences, on the other hand, are about helping our children understand the natural outcomes of their actions. They're not about making our kids feel bad, but about guiding them to make better choices in the future. We want to connect the dots between actions and consequences in a way that's fair and makes sense to them.

So, how do we nail this parenting tactic? It's all about our mindset when we're dealing with missteps. When your child acts out, take a moment. Ask yourself, "Am I trying to teach them something or just punish them?" This little pause can shift your approach from just doling out a penalty to actually guiding and teaching.

Remember, parenting isn't a battle to be won. It's about helping your child navigate their feelings and decisions. When we clearly understand the difference between consequences and punishment, we're not just enforcing rules; we're creating a nurturing environment, ripe for learning and personal growth.

By choosing to respond with consequences rather than punishment, we teach our children to consider their actions thoughtfully. We demonstrate how to navigate life with understanding and empathy, not fear and frustration.

On the next page are some examples of punishment versus consequences:

Behavior	Punishment (Traditional Way)	Consequences (Realistic & Understandable Approach)
Disrespectful language	Mouth washed out with soap	No video games until they speak kindly for a day
Incomplete chores	Sent to bed early	Can't go to a friend's house until their room is cleaned
Property damage	Spanked and grounded	Helps fix or clean what they damaged
Poor manners at dinner	No TV	Asked to leave the table, can return when ready to be polite
Lying	Sit in the corner facing the wall	Has to do extra small tasks to show they're trustworthy again
Stealing	Yelled at and lectured	Returns the item and apologizes to the person they stole from
Poor academic performance	Grounded at home	Extra study time set aside each evening until grades improve

"YELLING SILENCES YOUR
MESSAGE. SPEAK QUIETLY
SO YOUR CHILDREN CAN
HEAR YOUR WORDS INSTEAD
OF JUST YOUR VOICE."
– ANONYMOUS

@NOYELLINGPARENTINGTOOLBOX

C H A P T E R 4

NO-YELLING FORMULA

I magine a world of parenting where your voice stays calm, your child listens, and every challenge becomes an opportunity for growth and connection. Welcome to the No-Yelling Formula. This isn't just about yelling less. It's about a transformation in communication that turns every parenting moment into a positive experience.

Think of it as a script for successful parenting. Like actors with a well-rehearsed script, this formula sets the stage for smoother interactions, which foster understanding, connection, and growth with your kids.

Now, let's delve into why you need this formula. Parenting without this guidance can lead to ineffective and stressful situations. When your child refuses to clean their room or throws a tantrum, what's your instinct? If you're like many, you might raise your voice, hoping to be heard over the noise. But parenting isn't about quick fixes. Yelling might seem effective in the moment, but it can leave a bitter taste for all involved.

The No-Yelling Formula, also referred to as a mindful response, is like your manual for parenting, helping you identify your natural communication style and offering steps to improve it. Are you a yeller? Do you get frustrated easily? This formula helps you to minimize meltdowns for both you and your child, reduce conflict, and increase cooperation. It's about learning to mix firmness with love, patience, and understanding, to create the perfect blend for effective communication.

Let's explore how to handle parenting challenges without raising your voice and discover the magic of the No-Yelling Formula.

How to Talk to Your Child

If we didn't learn to manage our emotions effectively in our own childhood, we might often find ourselves repeating negative patterns. This often leads to moments where we express anger or mistakenly blame our children. It's a cycle where emotional control wasn't mastered early on, so it continues to challenge us in parenthood.

Thankfully, this cycle can be broken, and I'm here to show you how with four practical steps. Think of these four steps as a secret code. When you're talking with your kids, keep this code in mind. It'll help you catch those sneaky, negative words before they slip out.

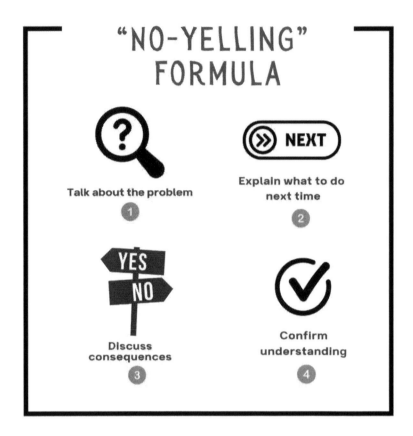

Step 1: Talk about the problem

State the problem or concern:

Let's use managing screen time as our example. Instead of the typical, "You're always on that iPad! I'm going to hide it!" or "That's it, you're doing extra chores for being glued to that screen," try a different approach.

You: "**I've noticed** that you seem to have trouble turning off the iPad when I ask. Let's talk about that.

It's simple, right? This approach is only stating the problem without the emotional heat. Sure, it feels different, but it's also effective. It moves the conversation from confrontational to collaborative. It's not about launching an attack; it's about bringing up a problem you both can solve together.

And here's a pro tip: keep a friendly smile on your face. Yes, it's tough, but it signals that you're open to a constructive conversation, not just laying down the law. This approach sets a respectful tone and clear expectations without ramping up the tension.

Step 2: Explain what to do next time

State the expected behavior and be clear about your expectations:

You: "I'd like you to turn off the iPad when I ask, without fuss."

This step is about setting crystal clear expectations. You're not just laying down rules; you're guiding your child towards responsible behavior. It's important they understand that these gadgets are a privilege. By stating, "I expect you to do it," you're highlighting what you *want* to see, not just what you don't want. The addition, "without fuss," is key. It clarifies that you're looking for compliance with a positive attitude. Be clear but also flexible, especially with younger kids. The goal is mutual respect and cooperation, not just rule enforcement.

Step 3: Discuss consequences

Reveal the consequences clearly and why it's important:

You: "If you don't turn off the iPad when asked, you'll have to take a break from it for a while."

This is where you lay out the boundaries and consequences. By saying, "If this happens again," you're giving a heads-up – it's their chance to choose the right behavior. The consequence, like a week without games, directly relates to the issue and helps your child see the link between actions and outcomes. Remember, **consistency is key**. If you say it, mean it. This teaches responsibility and respect for rules.

Step 4: Confirm understanding

Finally, ask your child to repeat the rules:

You: (Using a low, friendly, and soft voice) "Can you tell me what we've agreed about screen time?"

Tone is everything here. You're not a dictator; you're a guide. This step is like closing the loop. When your child repeats the rules and consequences, it confirms they've understood. Think of it as a casual recap, ensuring everyone's on the same page. This isn't about memorizing rules but understanding them. It's a way to reinforce responsibility and respect for boundaries.

Why Kids Don't Listen

When our kids test our patience, it's worth reflecting on how we handle it. Have you ever stopped to think about it? Here's a key thing to keep in mind: be reasonable. This simple concept is huge in parenting, especially when it comes to setting consequences. Imagine setting rules that are fair and make sense, just like you'd want at your own job. That's being reasonable.

It's not about being strict or soft, but about being fair. If your kid breaks a rule, the consequence should fit the mistake. Too harsh, and it's just unfair. Too soft, and the lesson gets lost. It's like finding the right volume on your music player – not too loud, not too quiet, but just right.

Next, we'll dive into the art of being reasonable. Remember, your child will thrive under your guidance when you listen, understand, and set clear, fair boundaries.

1. Respecting Your Child

The idea of respecting children might initially seem odd to some parents. "Respect for someone so little?" they might ask. "Why?" But respect isn't just for adults. It's crucial for the little ones too. Children, no matter how young, are surprisingly perceptive. They feel deeply, just like us. So, respect is about recognizing their feelings, their presence – respecting them as a person. It means not belittling their emotions or making them feel small. It's about treating them with kindness and understanding, showing them that they matter. After all, respect is a two-way street, and it starts from the earliest years, shaping how they see themselves and the world around them.

2. No Blame, Shame, or Pain

Consider a simple scenario: you spill something. As an adult, you'd likely clean it up and move on. But when a child makes a mess, our instinct might be to lecture them. Instead, we should handle their mistakes as we would our own. A response like, "Oops, that's okay. Let's clean it up together," teaches children that mistakes are manageable and not catastrophic.

Now, let's talk about the tougher stuff – like when they're not playing nice or they talk back. It's tempting to correct them right there in the heat of the moment. But consider this: how would you feel being called out in front of others? Pretty embarrassing, right? Kids feel that too. So, instead of a public tell-off, take them aside for a calm chat. It's about addressing the behavior without making them feel small. This approach shows them respect and helps them understand the why behind your guidance.

Remember, children learn best in an environment where they feel safe, loved, and valued, not one where they are humiliated, scared or threatened.

3. Reasonable Consequences

When it comes to parenting, giving consequences for misbehavior is more of an art than a science. The golden rule is to make sure the consequence is directly related to the behavior. Why? Because as parents, our ultimate goal is not just to discipline, but to promote genuine understanding and learning.

Scenario: Your child keeps riding their bike without a helmet. You might be tempted to pull out a random consequence that doesn't connect to the behavior.

Unrelated to misbehavior: "If you don't wear a helmet now, I won't let you watch TV."

But wait, what does TV have to do with bike safety? It's like comparing apples to oranges. Such unrelated consequences can end up confusing and even angering your child, and they won't really get the message you're trying to send.

For a consequence to really work and be fair, it needs to directly tie into the misbehavior. If the connection isn't there, kids might feel it's unfair and, therefore, not learn from it. They need to see a clear cause and effect.

Related to misbehavior: "If you don't wear your helmet, you won't be able to ride your bike for the next week."

Now, that's a consequence that makes sense. As you can see, it directly links the misbehavior (not wearing a helmet) with a related outcome (no biking).

This way, your child can learn that not wearing a helmet has consequences, reinforcing the importance of safety. Once the consequence matches their misbehavior, kids are more likely to take it to heart and change their behavior.

Next time you're faced with a misbehavior and need to enforce a consequence, remember to keep it relevant. The goal is to create a learning experience that sticks with your child.

4. Realistic & Manageable

When giving consequences for your child's actions, think about keeping them realistic and manageable. Going overboard with harsh or lengthy punishments can backfire, making them tough to stick to for both of you, and potentially damaging trust. Instead, aim for shorter, more achievable consequences that you can consistently enforce. This approach helps maintain trust and effectively teaches valuable lessons.

Consider the helmet scenario again:

Unreasonable duration: "No helmet? Then you're grounded from your bike for a whole month."

Hold up! Doesn't that sound a bit extreme? Is a whole month without the bike a fair tradeoff for not wearing a helmet? Probably not, particularly for younger kids. In the heat of the moment, such a lengthy consequence might slip out, but realistically, sticking to it for a whole month is a tall order.

Now, let's think about a more manageable and fair approach:

Reasonable duration: "If you refuse the helmet, then no bike riding for a week [or perhaps a day for a younger child]."

This makes way more sense. The consequence is directly related to the misbehavior, and the timeframe is something you can actually enforce without too much hassle. Your child will quickly grasp that not wearing a helmet leads to an immediate and related outcome.

The key here is to use consequences as *teaching tools*, not as a way to highlight every small mistake. By keeping the duration of consequences reasonable and tailored to your child's age and maturity level, you're more likely to follow through with them. And your child is more likely to understand, learn, and grow from the experience. It turns the whole dynamic into a positive learning opportunity for everyone involved.

In parenting, being reasonable is your secret weapon. It's the key to unlocking a world where understanding, cooperation, and growth thrive.

Kids are Understanding

As we explore the No-Yelling Formula, learn how to set fair consequences, and respond mindfully, there's one more important thing to keep in mind: kids are a lot more understanding than we sometimes think. It might surprise you, especially on those days filled with a little too much chaos and mischief. But remember, even when they're being a handful, kids can make sense of things pretty well if we just take the time to explain.

Imagine this: you're swamped with a big project at home, the deadline is breathing down your neck, and just then, your kids start playing loudly and rowdily in the living room. Instead of raising your voice, try a different approach. Calmly explain, "I really need to focus for the next couple of hours. How about you play outside or quietly with your blocks? Then, when I'm done, we can play a game together." This way, they understand what's going on and why it's important. Plus, they get to look forward to having your full attention later on.

You'll find that when you talk to them reasonably, they usually listen and even want to help. So next time things get hectic, remember, a little patience and a calm chat can go a long way. The kids will appreciate it, and you might just enjoy some peace and quiet to finish your work. Plus, there's the added bonus of time together, having fun and creating memories.

PART 3

STRATEGIES FOR KIDS' TANTRUMS

As parents, breaking free from the cycle of anger can be challenging. We often find ourselves at a loss for words or unsure how to react during our child's tantrum. This leads to default responses like yelling or punishing – reactions we later regret. That's exactly why I put together this book: to offer you a toolbox of strategies to become a calmer, more composed parent.

The way you respond to your child's tantrum is super important because kids will remember and mirror your reactions. Think about it: do we want our children to grow up unable to control their emotions, resorting to anger and screaming? Of course not. We all desire to raise individuals who can communicate effectively and manage their emotions in a healthy way.

Consider the role of warm-ups in physical activities like working out or swimming. Warm-ups prepare our muscles, increase flexibility, and minimize the risk of injuries. Similarly, the No-Yelling Formula acts as a warm-up for our parenting skills. It prepares us to be flexible and approach our child's anger calmly and with the right mindset.

Let's start seeing our kids as young individuals needing guidance, not just as troublemakers. Our role as parents is to guide them towards making better choices, especially during challenging moments like tantrums.

"WHEN LITTLE PEOPLE ARE
OVERWHELMED BY BIG
EMOTIONS, IT'S OUR JOB
TO SHARE OUR CALM, NOT
JOIN THEIR CHAOS."
– L.R. KNOST

@NOYELLINGPARENTINGTOOLBOX

C H A P T E R 5

PUBLIC TANTRUMS

You've been there, right? Those unforgettable moments with your little one – whether at a restaurant, grocery store, park, or family gathering – when, out of the blue, they decide to perform an Oscar-worthy tantrum. It feels like you're in the middle of a dramatic movie, with all eyes on you as you juggle your groceries and a screaming child. For any parent, it's a nightmare scenario.

Before becoming a parent, I thought such outbursts were just for the movies. But then my son came along and showed me the reality of parenting – complete with its fair share of public tantrums.

Handling these outbursts in public can be a real challenge. They can leave us feeling embarrassed, pressured to give in, or wishing we could just disappear. However, as tough as they are, it's important to remember that tantrums are a normal part of a child's development. They often stem from a child's frustration or their struggle to communicate needs and feelings.

In this chapter, we're going to dive deep into public tantrums. We'll explore why they happen, how to handle them effectively, plus the dos and don'ts to keep in mind. I'll also share a scripted exercise that illustrates a practical approach to managing these challenging moments. Let's get started!

Decoding Tantrums

Picture this: you're in a bustling store, and suddenly, your child is on the floor, kicking and screaming. Your first thought? "Here we go again." But let's pause and see it in a new light. This meltdown isn't just about making a scene – it's like your child is sending an S.O.S. in a language you're still figuring out. So, to better understand why tantrums occur, let's decode some of the secret signals children send through their behavior and discern the real message behind those tears and screams. Here are some common tantrum triggers:

- **Tiredness:** Ever felt so tired you could cry? Kids feel that too. When they're wiped out, a tantrum might be their way of saying, "I need a nap, like, now!" Remember that time at the family BBQ when little Sam just lost it? It might've been past his naptime.

- **Sensory Overload:** The world's a big, noisy place, and for tiny tots, it can get overwhelming. Bright lights, loud noises, or just too many people can all be a bit too much. Think of those shopping trips when the mall is buzzing, and suddenly, your little one's had enough.
- **Hunger:** We've all been there – that moment when you're so hungry you're on edge. Kids feel that "hangry" rush too. Those pre-dinner meltdowns could be your kiddo's way of saying, "I'm starving!"
- **Frustration:** Imagine trying to tie your shoelaces, but your fingers just won't cooperate. That's a day in the life of a toddler. Wanting to do something but not quite managing – it's frustrating and could be the trigger for tears.
- **Attention Seeking:** Kids need to feel noticed and valued. Sometimes, a tantrum is their loudspeaker, saying, "Hey, I'm here, and I need a hug!" Remember when little Emma threw a fit at the park? She might've just been looking for a bit more of your time and love.

Understanding Through Observation

- **Silent Conversations:** Observe the small signs – a yawn that says "I'm sleepy," little hands balled up in frustration, or a puzzled frown. These silent signals can speak volumes.
- **Emotional Wave**: Remember, kids ride a roller coaster of feelings, but they're still learning the ropes on how to handle them. Their emotions strike fast and run deep, and they need our help to navigate through them.
- **Parenting Detectives:** Observe your child and identify what triggers the tantrums. Does the chaos of a crowded place set them off? Does missing a nap lead to meltdowns? You're collecting clues to solve the mystery of their outbursts.

- **Empathy is Key:** Sometimes, all it takes is a gentle, "I see you're upset. Let's figure this out together." It's almost like a secret spell that transforms a meltdown into a moment of connection and learning, teaching them about their emotions and how to express them.

It's essential to show children that tantrums won't get them what they want. Instead, encourage them to express their feelings constructively. From about age 3, start teaching them to identify and name their emotions. For example, "I see you're angry about having to eat veggies, but they're important to make you healthy and strong," helps them label their feelings and learn how to manage them. But even before age 3, naming emotions for a child can help them feel seen and understood.

As children grow, especially into their school years, you'll likely notice a decrease in tantrums. This is because they're learning more effective ways to communicate and resolve conflicts. However, be prepared for a possible resurgence during the tumultuous teenage years. The complexities of teenage emotions can reignite tantrum-like behaviors. Teaching them emotional management skills early on can be invaluable for navigating these challenging years.

In summary, managing tantrums involves understanding unspoken signals and guiding your child through their emotional growth. It's about helping them develop into emotionally intelligent individuals who can navigate their feelings in healthy ways.

What To Do During A Tantrum

Handling a child's tantrum can feel like navigating a storm – it's chaotic and overwhelming. Remember, tantrums are a part of your child's journey of self-discovery, and how you respond can make all the difference.

1. Keep calm

I get it – keeping calm during a tantrum is easier said than done. Your emotions and tension run nearly as high as your child's, and keeping yourself calm can seem impossible. I understand this, but here's a tip: take a deep breath. Count to five or ten, whatever it takes to give yourself a moment. This small pause helps you regain composure and approach the situation more rationally. Remind yourself, "I can handle this," to boost your confidence and calm.

2. Eye contact (Don't glare at the child with anger)

Facing your little one in full mischief mode can be tough. You might not feel like making eye contact when they're testing your patience, but remember, you're the adult in the room. Your reaction sets the tone.

You probably want to show how angry you are and may be tempted to shoot a laser beam from your eyes so your child can feel the anger. But let's hit pause. That's not the way we want to navigate these waters. Instead, opt for calm, gentle eye contact. No hint of anger, just a soft, understanding gaze. Your child shouldn't feel intimidated by Mom or Dad. They need to see that you're addressing their actions, not attacking them personally. Let your eyes speak with love, guiding them to understand where they've gone astray.

3. Hug it out

Never underestimate the power of a hug. Just like a warm embrace can diffuse tension between adults, it can work wonders with your child as well. Offering a hug during a tantrum isn't giving in; it's providing comfort. It's a silent message that they're safe and loved, easing their emotional turmoil. So, next time your child is in the middle of a tantrum, don't hesitate to offer a nice, warm hug.

4. Change the scenery

Sometimes, all you need is a change of scenery to hit the reset button on a tense situation. If the root of the tantrum is lingering in the background, stepping into a new space can make all the difference. As you change the environment, engage your child with a distraction – point out something interesting or start a light conversation. This helps both of you to break free from the tantrum's grip.

5. Don't worry about other people

In public, it's easy to worry about what others think, but your focus should be solely on your child. Tantrums are a normal part of child development. Remember, every parent has been there. Most onlookers are likely to empathize rather than judge.

When you find yourself dealing with a public tantrum, let go of the worries about what other people might think and channel your energy into helping your child manage their emotions. Your main focus is to guide and support your child through this learning moment.

Parenting Challenge

Below, I present a common scenario to help you practice the No-Yelling Formula. Try to picture yourself in each situation.

I've given two reactions: the typical response and a more desired, mindful approach.

Scenario: You're in a grocery store with your 4-year-old daughter, Jamie. She spots a candy bar at the checkout and asks for it. You refuse, and she starts crying loudly, attracting attention.

Typical Response:

Parent (frustrated): "Why can't you ever behave? No more grocery store trips if you keep crying!"

Jamie (crying): "But I want it! I want it!"

Parent: "That's it, we're leaving. You're in trouble when we get home!"

Result: This reaction only escalates the situation. The parent feels embarrassed and angry, while Jamie feels misunderstood and overlooked. It's a lose-lose scenario, leaving both parent and child upset and disconnected.

Improved Mindful Response: Let's apply the No-Yelling Formula.

— Step 1: Talk about the problem.

Start with observational phrases like "I've noticed" or "I see" or "I understand."

Parent (calmly): "Jamie, **I've noticed that** you often ask for treats when we're at the store."

Jamie (crying): "It's because I really, really want that candy!"

— Step 2: Explain what to do next time.

State the expected behavior and give a clear instruction.

Parent: "I understand, but we can't have a tantrum every time mommy says no, especially at the checkout. **Next time, let's try this:** ask me nicely before we get to the checkout, and we'll talk about whether it's okay or not."

Jamie: (sniffing and wiping her tears): "Okay, but can I have it now?"

— Step 3: Discuss consequences.

State what will happen if the behavior is repeated.

Parent: "No, honey, not this time. And remember, if this happens again, we will have to skip our fun activity after shopping. It's not a punishment; it's about learning to make good choices."

Jamie: "Okay. I'll try to do better."

— Step 4: Confirm understanding.

Ask the child to repeat back what you discussed.

Parent: "Great, Jamie. Can you repeat our agreement?"

Jamie: "Ask nicely for treats, or we miss out on fun activities."

Parent: "Exactly, Jamie. I'm glad you understand."

Result: The situation is resolved with less tension. Jamie feels heard and learns the importance of calm discussion. The No-Yelling Formula is effectively applied.

Whether you're in a park, local store, family gathering, or anywhere else, remember the calm way to navigate tantrums using the No-Yelling Formula. And if things don't go exactly like this scripted conversation, stay calm and try not to stress. It may take some practice on your part. Your child may not always go along so easily, but after a while, they too will begin to get the hang of the calmer approach and will be comforted to know you are in control of the situation. Tantrums are part of children's emotional development, and our guidance is crucial in these moments.

Reaction Training

Scenario 1: Restaurant Rebellion

During a family dinner at a restaurant, 5-year-old Aiden refuses to stay in his seat, continuously getting up and disrupting other diners.

Your Typical Reaction:

- Whispering sternly for Aiden to sit down.
- Feeling embarrassed and telling Aiden he's ruining dinner.
- Threatening to take away his dessert or a favorite toy as a consequence.

Now, let's transform this scenario, applying the No-Yelling Formula with a 4-step mindful response.

1. Talk about the problem

Take Aiden to a quiet corner and gently explain: "I notice that you're having trouble remaining seated. When you leave your seat and move around in the restaurant, it's not safe, and it disturbs other people who are also trying to enjoy their meals."

2. Explain what to do next time

"In restaurants, we need to stay in our seats. It shows respect to the other diners and the staff working here. Let's practice sitting together and enjoying our meal like those around us."

3. Discuss consequences

"I know sitting still can be tough, but it's important here. If you can't stay seated, we'll have to step outside until you're ready to behave, or it might mean no dessert today. It's about following the rules so everyone can enjoy their meal."

4. Confirm understanding

"So, tell me, what should we do when we're eating out?"

Aiden: "I need to stay in my chair and not run around."

Parent: "That's right, Aiden. I know you can do it. Thank you for understanding."

Scenario 2: Library Loudness

Now it's your turn. Read this scenario and think about your typical response. Next, try to formulate a more mindful response using the No-Yelling Formula.

While in a library, 2-year-old Mia starts crying at a high pitch because she can't take home all the books she wants to check out.

Your Typical Reaction:

_____

_____

_____

_____

_____

Your desired reaction applying the No-Yelling Formula, using a 4-Step Mindful Response:

_____

_____

_____

_____

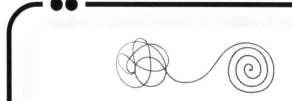

"DISCIPLINE IS HELPING A CHILD
SOLVE A PROBLEM. PUNISHMENT IS
MAKING A CHILD SUFFER FOR HAVING
A PROBLEM. TO RAISE PROBLEM-
SOLVERS, FOCUS ON SOLUTIONS NOT
RETRIBUTION." – L.R. KNOST

@NOYELLINGPARENTINGTOOLBOX

C H A P T E R 6

REFUSAL TO COOPERATE

F amily road trips can be both fun and challenging, especially with kids. Imagine this: you're all set for an exciting adventure, the car packed with snacks and excitement, but just before you hit the road, your 6-year-old refuses to buckle up. Frustrating, right?

Well, in this chapter, we're diving into the world of dealing with kids who won't cooperate. It's like a twist in the plot of your family adventure. But don't worry, we'll uncover the secrets to turning these challenging moments into opportunities for growth and connection. So, buckle up yourself, and let's get started on this journey!

First, let's assess your current approach to dealing with your child's refusal to cooperate. On a scale of 1–5, with 5 being the most frequent, rate yourself on the following statements:

1. I often find myself in power struggles with my child.
2. I tend to say "no" to my child frequently.
3. I believe offering choices can be an effective way to handle refusal to cooperate.

Upon reviewing your scores: High marks in power struggles or frequent "no" answers suggest a need for new strategies to reduce conflict. High scores in offering choices reflect a positive approach towards encouraging cooperation. Reflect and adjust as needed for smoother interactions.

Power Struggles

Power struggles are arguments you have with your kids when you both want different things. Imagine telling your child to clean their room, and they keep saying "No." You say "You have to do it now," but they still refuse. This is a power struggle – you both are trying to be the boss.

Again: you tell your child to turn off the TV and do their homework. They want to keep watching, so they might start to argue or even throw a fit. The more you push, the more they push back, leading to frustration for everyone involved.

In these moments, it can feel like your child is trying to see how much they can get away with. You might think you need to be extra strict to show you're the boss. But this can just make your child act out more.

Power struggles are just part of being a family. They happen because you and your child have different ideas about what should happen. Remember, it's not just about making your child do what you say. It's about understanding why they might not want to do it, helping them understand why you want them to, and finding a way to work it out together.

Here's how to smartly handle power struggles:

Rule #1 - Avoid power struggles when possible: Don't get into a fight over every minor issue. If it's not a big deal, let it go.

- Example: If your child wants to wear a mismatched outfit, it might not be worth arguing about. It's a harmless way for them to express themselves.

Rule #2 - Win power struggles wisely: Sometimes, despite your best efforts, you'll find yourself in a power struggle with your child. When this happens, remember to keep cool and help your child think of a good choice.

- Example: Your child refuses to clean their room. Instead of losing your temper, take a deep breath and try a different approach. Offer choices like, "Would you like to clean your room now and have extra playtime later, or first play for 15 minutes and clean up after?" This approach promotes positive behavior, patience, and decision-making.

Rule #3 - Pick your battles: Focus on important issues that you *must* control. This way, you avoid unnecessary arguments and focus on what matters.

- Example: If your teenager wants to dye their hair, consider if it's a battle worth having. If it's just a hair color and not harmful, you might let them make that choice. However, if the issue is about something that affects their health or safety, like not wearing a seatbelt, that's a battle worth picking.

Two good choices

A simple yet effective parenting strategy to reduce power struggles involves preventing your child from defaulting to "No." The strategy is straightforward: don't ask questions that can be answered with a simple "YES" or "NO." This technique is about giving two acceptable options, allowing your child to make a choice.

To make this strategy work, tweak how you frame your requests. Instead of commands that might trigger a "No," give two choices that lead to the outcome you want. Here's how you could do it in everyday language:

- Joining In: Instead of "Are you coming or not?" try "Do you wanna wear your red shoes or your blue ones when we go out?"
- Listening Up: Instead of "Can you please pay attention to me when I am talking?" say "Do you want to chat about this now, or in five minutes after you're done with your game?"
- Snack Time: Instead of "Can you return the snack to the rack?" ask "Would you like to help me put this back, or pick out what we'll have for snack tomorrow?"
- Laundry Help: Instead of "Please help put the clothes in the laundry basket," go with "Do you want to throw the clothes into the basket like a basketball player, or carry them over like a strongman?"
- Homework Time: Instead of just saying "Do your homework," try "What's first today: math or reading?"
- Phone at the Table: Instead of "Can you please stop using your phone when at the dining table?" offer "Do you want to check

your phone quickly before we eat, or wait until after we're done?"

Putting It into Practice

After shifting away from direct commands, the next step is to engage your child with choices that encourage cooperation without needing to explain the reasons extensively, nag, negotiate, or repeat yourself. Once you've captured your child's attention, present two appealing options. This empowers them to make decisions within boundaries they're comfortable with. Remember, simplicity and clarity are key to making sure they understand and follow through.

For younger kids, the choices should be straightforward and directly relate to their immediate world:

- "Do you want pizza or mac 'n' cheese for lunch?"
- "Would you rather play at the playground or visit the library today?"
- "After lunch, how about watching a movie or going to the park?"
- "What's your pick for today: white shorts or blue jeans?"

For older kids, the options can involve more complex decision-making and consequences:

- "Getting a new phone could be your birthday present, or if you prefer it sooner, you could cover half the cost with your savings. We could also think about a garage sale or a lemonade stand to help with expenses."
- "For your room cleaning, would you like to take care of it yourself, or use $50 from your allowance to hire a cleaning service?"

By framing your guidance in this manner, not only do you avoid potential pushback, but you also foster your child's ability to make thoughtful decisions and take responsibility for their choices.

Let's test your knowledge about the "Two Good Choices" strategy. Answer the following questions to see how well you understand this approach:

1: What is the main goal of offering two good choices to your child?
   a) To micromanage their decisions
   b) To promote independence and decision-making
   c) To limit their choices
   d) To avoid giving any options

2: When implementing this strategy, what should you avoid doing?
   a) Offering clear instructions
   b) Explaining the reasons behind the choices
   c) Nagging and negotiating
   d) Repeating yourself
   e) b, c, d

3: Can you provide an example of offering two good choices for an older child? (Answer in the space below)

The correct answers are: 1) b, and 2) e. Remember, the goal isn't to micromanage every aspect of your child's life but to equip them with the values and skills needed for independent thriving.

How to Get Your Kids to Listen

As parents, we often find ourselves saying "No" a lot, but what if we shifted our focus from what's wrong to what's right? The word *no* tends to highlight the problem, not the solution. And let's face it, after hearing "No" a thousand times, it starts to lose its impact on kids. They might even start tuning it out.

Why not try being more positive? This simple change can really lighten up the whole vibe at home. The trick is to say "Yes" more often, redirecting requests in a positive way without losing sight of your parenting goals.

Transforming "No" into "Yes":

Before saying "No," pause and think about how you can turn it into a "Yes." Here are some examples:

- Instead of "No, you can't have pizza tonight," say "Yes, let's plan for pizza tomorrow night!"
- Replace "No, you can't go to Kevin's house today" with "Yes, you can visit Kevin this weekend."
- Change "No, you can't play video games now" to "Yes, you can have some video game time this weekend after homework is done."

When your kids realize what's happening, they might try to push for immediate gratification. If they say, "But I want it now," just calmly repeat your "Yes" statement. Getting into a debate defeats the purpose. Stick to your positive approach, and you'll see a change in no time.

Here are more positive approaches:

- Park Scenario: Rather than, "No more fussing! Get in the stroller!" try "Let's plan our next fun park visit!"
- Mealtime Manners: If your child throws food, instead of "No throwing food," ask, "Are you done with your meal?" and then remove the food.
- Bedtime Reading: For requests for more bedtime stories, instead of "No more books tonight," offer, "We'll read this book first thing tomorrow morning!"

- Busy Parent: If your child wants to be picked up while you're busy, instead of "No, I can't right now," say, "I'll hold you as soon as I finish this task."

Parenting Challenge

Scenario: It's 7:00 a.m. on a Monday, and your 7-year-old son, Alex, is still in pajamas, playing with toys. Despite being reminded to get dressed for school multiple times, he remains unmoved.

Typical Response:

Parent (frustrated): "Alex, how many times must I tell you to get dressed?"

Alex: "But I don't want to go to school today."

Parent (raising voice): "Hurry up, or you're going to school in your pajamas!"

Alex (upset): "You always shout at me!"

Result: We already know what will happen after this. The situation escalates and the parent and kid start their day in a bad mood. While Alex feels unheard and pressured, the parent fumes with anger and frustration.

Improved Mindful Response: Apply the No-Yelling Formula.

— Step 1: Talk about the problem

Parent: **"I've noticed** that you're still not ready for school. It's important to follow our morning schedule to avoid being late."

Alex: "I just wanted to play more."

— Step 2: Explain what to do next time

Parent: "Playing is fine, but let's make a plan. Tidy up, get dressed, then eat breakfast. If you're quick, you can play a bit before leaving. Sound good?"

Alex: "Okay, I'll try."

— Step 3: Discuss consequences

Parent: "Remember, if you're not ready on time tomorrow, we will have to skip morning playtime, and toys will stay away until after school. We don't want you to miss anything at school."

Alex: "I don't want to miss out."

— Step 4: Confirm understanding

Parent: "Can you summarize our plan for the morning?"

Alex: "I should get ready for school, then I can play for a bit. If I'm not timely, no playtime, and toys are away until after school. I shouldn't be late."

Parent: "Exactly, Alex. I'm glad you understand."

Result: This approach addresses the issue calmly, providing positive motivation and clear expectations, leading to a cooperative and constructive outcome.

Reaction Training

Scenario 1: Morning Routine Delays

Seven-year-old Lucas consistently delays getting dressed in the morning, often leading to a rush to get ready for school.

Your Typical Reaction:

- Constant reminders for Lucas to get dressed while preparing breakfast.
- Growing frustration, raising your voice: "You're going to be late again!"
- Eventually hurrying him to get dressed quickly to avoid tardiness.

Your desired reaction applying the No-Yelling Method with a 4-Step mindful response:

1. Talk about the problem

"Lucas, **I've noticed** we're often late in the mornings because getting dressed takes a long time. We need to fix this."

2. Explain what to do next time

"**Next time,** let's get dressed right after you wake up. It'll make our mornings go smoother."

3. Discuss consequences

"If getting dressed still takes too long, we will have to skip your morning cartoons. Quick dressing means more fun time!"

4. Confirm understanding

"What's our new morning plan, and what happens if getting dressed takes too long?"

Lucas: "I'll get dressed as soon as I wake up. If I take too long, I might miss cartoon time."

Parent: "Right. Let's make our mornings better together. Thanks, Lucas!"

Scenario 2: Refusal to Clean Up

Now it's your turn. Consider the following scene and think about your typical reaction, then imagine a more mindful response, following the No-Yelling Formula.

After playing with her toys, 6-year-old Ava refuses to put them away, even after being asked multiple times.

Your Typical Reaction:

_____

_____

_____

_____

_____

_____

Your desired reaction using the No-Yelling Formula with a 4-Step Mindful Response:

_____

_____

_____

_____

"WHEN YOU FEEL ANGER RISING,
REMIND YOURSELF THAT PEACE
IS A CHOICE, AND ASK
YOURSELF IF THIS MOMENT OF
ANGER IS REALLY WORTH
SACRIFICING YOUR PEACE."
– ANONYMOUS

@NOYELLINGPARENTINGTOOLBOX

C H A P T E R 7

IGNORING INSTRUCTIONS

I magine that you walk into your sitting room and see your child's school shoes littered on the floor while they play video games. You ask your child to put their shoes away, but you get ignored. You repeat yourself, but still there is no response. Before you know what's happened, you find yourself angry and yelling.

Has something similar happened to you? We all know how frustrating it can be when kids ignore our instructions, even after we've repeated ourselves several times. Although we start out calm, impatience gets the better of us and, eventually, we may find ourselves screaming in hopes of being heard. That's not productive for anyone.

This chapter aims to tackle common scenarios where parents' instructions are disregarded, despite trying to communicate calmly. The goal is to move away from the frustration of ignored instructions and toward a mutual understanding that when you give instruction, your child will follow it.

Why Kids Don't Listen

Have you ever asked your child to do something and gotten... silence? Parents can feel invisible sometimes. But there's more to it than just kids being kids. In this section, we'll delve into the reasons why our words sometimes seem to disappear into a void. Often, you're dealing with your kids' growing desire for independence, their feeling overwhelmed from too many instructions, and their living in the moment. Also, the way we communicate with them makes a difference. By understanding these factors, we can transform moments of silence into opportunities for deeper connection and growth. Let's now delve into the reasons behind such behavior.

1. Seeking Independence

Why It Happens:

Often, kids ignore instructions as a way of asserting their indepen-dence. They're not just being difficult; they're learning to make their own choices, a crucial skill for their development.

Practical Tip:

Help them feel like they're in charge of some of their choices. When you need them to do something, give them options. For example, at bedtime, instead of just saying "Go brush your teeth," ask them, "What do you want to do first, brush your teeth or put on pajamas?" This way, they get to decide something on their own, and you still get them to do what's needed.

2. Instruction Overload

Why It Happens:

Children can get overwhelmed by too many instructions. Their brains are still developing, and processing a list of tasks can be challenging. When they ignore instructions, it might be because they don't know where to start or what to prioritize.

Practical Tip:

Simplify tasks and instructions. Break down tasks into smaller, more manageable steps. For instance, instead of saying, "Clean your room," you could say, "Let's start by putting the toys in the toy box," making the task more manageable.

3. The "Now" Factor

Why It Happens:

Kids live in the "now." If they don't see why they should do something right this second, it might not seem important. Telling them to clean their room because guests are coming over next week is like telling them about next year's Christmas. It's too far away for them to care.

Practical Tip:

Link instructions to immediate, relatable outcomes. Instead of touting abstract benefits by saying, "Do your homework so you'll do well in school," try, "Finish your homework now for extra playtime later."

4. Are We Speaking Their Language?

Why It Happens:

Sometimes the way we talk to our kids might as well be in Martian. If we're too complicated, too serious, or too "lecture-y," we lose them. We need to get down to their level, make it fun, or at least understandable.

Practical Tip:

Use simple, one or two-step instructions and turn the task into a challenge that they might enjoy. For instance, by saying, "I wonder how quickly you can put away the train set," you make it sound like a fun game. This approach motivates them more effectively, as it relates the task to something they care about and introduces an element of play. Who knows, we might just get them to listen and even enjoy it.

Effective Communication

Clear communication is essential when interacting with your children. Let's look at a common scenario involving watching TV to emphasize the importance of clarity.

Original Scenario:

Child: "Mom/Dad, can I watch the TV, please?"

Parent: "Of course you can, but make sure it's not too loud."

The child increases the volume, leading to repeated requests from the parent to lower it, which are ignored, culminating in frustration and the TV being turned off.

Issue: The instruction "keep it down" lacks specificity, making it hard for the child to follow.

Solution: Use concrete, specific instructions and establish clear, immediate consequences for non-compliance.

Revised Scenario:

Child: "Mom/Dad, can I watch the TV, please?"

Parent: "Sure, but the volume needs to stay at level 15. If it goes above that, we'll have a quick reminder. If it happens again, the TV goes off for the rest of the day. Deal?"

The child agrees and initially keeps the volume at the agreed level. After a while, the volume increases beyond the set limit.

Parent: "I noticed the volume is higher than we agreed. Let's turn it back to 15, please."

The child lowers the volume but later increases it again.

Parent: "We had an agreement about the volume. Since it's been raised again, we need to follow through with our consequences. It's time to turn off the TV for today."

This approach not only sets a clear expectation, but also involves the child in the agreement, making them more accountable. By establishing immediate consequences and following through, the child learns the importance of adhering to agreements, and improving compliance and communication.

More examples of Vague versus Clear instructions:
- Vague: "You can play video games for a bit."
- Clear: "You have 30 minutes to play your video game. When the kitchen timer rings, it'll be time to turn it off and start your homework."

- Vague: "Dinner will be ready soon."
- Clear: "Dinner is at 7:00 p.m. Please wash your hands and be at the table by then."

- Vague: "Let's go see a movie later."
- Clear: "We're going to the cinema for the 3:00 p.m. showing of the latest Spider-Man movie. Please get ready to leave after lunch."

Consistency is crucial. Adhere to the timelines and rules you set. For example, if you give an hour for video games, respect that time. Timed reminders can also be helpful, like giving a 5-minute warning before transitioning to the next activity.

By consistently providing clear instructions, you not only reduce misunderstandings but also build trust and teach your children the importance of reliability and structure.

Need Extra Miles?

Taking immediate action doesn't mean you have to fall into a cycle of nagging, pleading, or repeating yourself. If the TV volume isn't lowered after your request, turn it off. If lunch lingers too long and jeopardizes plans, explain calmly that the opportunity is missed for today, but there's always next time.

Expect pushback when you enforce rules.
- **Stay calm:** A deep breath goes a long way. Tantrums are temporary. Your calm response teaches valuable lessons in managing emotions.

- **Expect resistance:** It's natural for children to push boundaries. This is their way of learning. By standing firm on consequences, you're showing the seriousness of your expectations.

- **Avoid yelling:** Yelling might be our first reaction when frustrated, but it often leads to kids tuning out or becoming defensive, making it less likely they'll listen or follow instructions promptly. A calm tone paired with straightforward guidance does wonders. It helps children grasp what's expected of them more clearly, increasing the chances they'll respond positively the first time you ask. This method not only fosters respect, but also promotes a more harmonious interaction, setting a foundation for effective communication and mutual understanding.

With consistent application of this approach, your child will gradually understand the link between actions and consequences. Typically, within a couple of weeks, you'll start to notice a positive change in their behavior. In most cases, they will begin to follow instructions more readily, recognizing that you are committed to enforcing the rules you've set. This shift doesn't happen overnight, but with patience and persistence, you'll see that your efforts to communicate effectively and maintain your calm are truly making a difference.

Parenting Challenges

Dealing with kids who ignore instructions is a common source of frustration. Let's look at a scripted scenario to compare ineffective and effective ways of managing such situations.

Scenario: A parent asks their 7-year-old son, Jake, to put away his game console and get ready for bed. Jake continues playing, ignoring the instructions.

Typical Response:

Parent: "Jake, put away your game console and get ready for bed."

Jake ignores and continues playing.

Parent (loudly): "Jake! Why don't you ever listen? Stop ignoring me!"

Jake (defensively): "I heard you! I just want to finish this game."

Result: The situation escalates, communication breaks down, and both parties feel frustrated.

Improved Mindful Response:

— Step 1: Talk about the problem

Parent: "**I've noticed that** you don't answer me but continue playing after I've asked you to put away your game console and get ready for bed."

Jake: "I just wanted to finish this game."

— Step 2: Explain what to do next time

Parent: "I see you're really into your game, and that's cool. **But for next time**, I need you to follow our bedtime routine, okay? Here's what I expect: when it's time, turn off the game, head to your room, brush your teeth, wash your face, and change into your pajamas. Can you remember to do all that?"

Jake: "I can try."

— Step 3: Discuss consequences

Parent: "I'm counting on you to handle this. But remember, if you don't follow through, then you won't be able to play video games after dinner for a week. We need to make sure you're getting enough sleep, alright?"

Jake: "Okay. I'll do better."

— Step 4: Confirm understanding

Parent: "Can you repeat what we agreed on, just to be sure?"

Jake: "I need to stop gaming at bedtime and get ready for bed. If I don't, no video games after dinner for a week."

Parent: "Exactly! I'm glad we understand each other."

Result: This approach leads to mutual understanding. Jake is aware of the consequences, and the parent has effectively communicated the expectations and consequences.

Reaction Training

Scenario 1: Bedtime Delays

Despite being told it's bedtime, 7-year-old Liam remains on the couch, engrossed in his favorite TV show, as if he never heard the instruction.

Your Typical Reaction:

- Repeatedly reminding Liam to turn off the TV.
- Raising your voice: "Liam, how many times do I have to tell you?"
- Eventually turning off the TV yourself, resulting in an argument or upset feelings.

Your desired reaction using the 4-Step Mindful Response:

Step 1: Talk about the problem

Parent: "Liam, I've noticed you find it hard to turn off the TV when it's bedtime."

Step 2: Explain what to do next time

Parent: "Here's our plan: When the clock shows 8 p.m., that's our signal to turn off the TV and start getting ready for bed. Can you manage that tonight?"

Step 3: Discuss consequences

Parent: "If the TV isn't turned off by 8 p.m., then tomorrow's TV time will be shortened by 15 minutes. It's important we stick to our bedtime routine for a good night's rest."

Step 4: Confirm understanding

Parent: "Liam, can you repeat what we've agreed about TV time and bedtime?"

Liam: "I turn off the TV at 8 p.m. If I don't, I get less TV time tomorrow."

Parent: "Exactly, Liam. I appreciate your cooperation. Following our schedule ensures we all get enough rest."

Scenario 2: Ignoring Safety Rules

Now it's your turn. Consider your typical reaction to the following scenario and record it below. Then think of a more mindful response and write it down.

Even after constant reminders to wear a helmet while cycling, 9-year-old Jake often rides his bike without it, dismissing the repeated safety warnings. Consider your typical response and record it here. Then practice a more mindful response below.

Your Typical Reaction:

_____

_____

_____

_____

_____

Your desired reaction using the 4-Step Mindful Response:

_____

_____

_____

_____

CUSTOMER REVIEW

Please Review My Book

I hope you're enjoying the book so far! If you have a moment, I'd love to hear your thoughts through a review. Your feedback is invaluable and helps me continue my work. Thank you for your support!"

Carrie Khang

"EVERY TIME YOU FEEL
YOURSELF GETTING ANGRY,
REMEMBER THAT YOUR CHILD
IS LEARNING HOW TO HANDLE
EMOTIONS FROM YOU."
– ANONYMOUS

@NOYELLINGPARENTINGTOOLBOX

C H A P T E R 8

DISRESPECTFUL BEHAVIOR

Picture a typical evening: you're busy cooking dinner, occasionally glancing over to make sure your child is doing their homework. For the umpteenth time, you've asked them to focus on getting their homework done, but each time, it is brushed aside as they ignore you and respond with dismissive gestures and eye rolls.

Immediately after what's meant to be yet another gentle reminder, your child snaps back at you, "You can't make me do anything. You're always nagging!" This sudden outburst not only hurts but also leaves you feeling frustrated and questioning where things went wrong.

Such disrespect from our kids can catch us off guard and test our patience and parenting skills. In this chapter, we will delve into these difficult situations. We'll explore why disrespectful behavior occurs and provide strategies to help you navigate and manage these incidents constructively. Our focus will be on transforming these challenging moments into opportunities for teaching respect and strengthening communication.

Common Disrespectful Behaviors

Dealing with disrespectful behavior from your kids can make you feel like you're walking on a minefield. You never know when you'll step on a trigger. Let's identify and understand some common disrespectful behaviors parents often face.

- **Constant Interruption:** Your child cuts into conversations without regard for others' speaking turns, leaving you bewildered about their impatience.
- **Ignoring Rules or Boundaries:** Your child repeatedly disobeys rules, testing limits and authority.
- **Talking Back:** A frequent challenge where children respond rudely or sassily to everything you say.

- **Using Inappropriate Language:** Despite clear boundaries, they use offensive or foul language, sometimes directed at others.
- **Mimicking or Mocking:** This is one quick button-pusher. They mockingly repeat what you say, turning conversations into frustrating exchanges.
- **Physical Disrespect:** It feels as if our little ones forget they're the kids and we are the adults. They may show disrespect by overstepping physical boundaries by pushing, hitting, or shoving, often to express dissent or frustration.
- **Disregarding Others' Feelings:** Laughing at someone else's misfortune, including yours, showing a lack of empathy.
- **Taking What Isn't Theirs:** This is when kids take things that don't belong to them without asking. It could be something from your purse or even a friend's stuff. They're not respecting that it's someone else's property.
- **Eye-rolling or Sighing:** Your child's nonverbal way of saying, "I don't want to listen to you," or "You are being ridiculous." They do this to signal annoyance or disdain towards guidance or instructions.

Each of these behaviors is not just an act of defiance, but also a communication of underlying needs and a way to test boundaries. As parents, we should decode these signals and guide them towards more respectful ways of expressing themselves and dealing with their emotions. Our goal is not merely to curb undesirable behaviors but to understand the root causes and teach healthier methods of interaction and emotional regulation.

Why Kids Need Boundaries

Setting boundaries for kids might seem tough, but it's actually really helpful for them. It's like giving them a map that shows them how to behave, especially when they're being disrespectful. Without these rules, kids might start thinking they're the boss, which causes an imbalance of authority.

For instance, say, it's bedtime, yet they throw a fit to watch TV instead. If the parent gives in, the kid starts thinking they're in charge and may begin lobbying for other situations that aren't healthy. Kids need boundaries to flourish both mentally and physically. Deep down, kids actually want to know their parents are steering the ship and keeping them safe.

When kids try to push against the rules, it's important that parents stand their ground. This doesn't mean being super strict all the time. It means making a home where kids feel secure and know there's someone in charge whom they can count on.

By setting clear rules, kids get to be kids. They know their parents will love them, help them, and keep them safe. These rules and what happens when they're not followed should be crystal clear – no confusion. If kids step out of line, sticking to the consequences is key.

So, what good things happen when we have clear boundaries?

- **Safety**: Kids feel safe when they know the rules. Like a rule that says, "No running near the pool," so they know how to be safe there.
- **Predictability:** When there's a routine, kids aren't surprised by what comes next. For example, having breakfast before school and doing homework before playtime helps them know what to expect.

- **Stability:** If rules aren't clear, kids may feel nervous because they don't know what's expected of them. Having consistent rules, like no phones at the dinner table, kids can relax what's expected, making mealtime a calm space for family chats.
- **Responsibility:** Rules teach kids to be responsible. A rule like "Clean up your toys" helps them learn to take care of their stuff.
- **Respect:** They learn to think about others. A rule like "Knock on your sibling's door before barging in" teaches them to respect others' spaces.
- **Freedom Within Limits:** When kids know the rules, they can explore and try new things safely. Letting them pick their clothes within certain guidelines (like dressing for the weather) helps them make choices on their own.
- **Independence**: Kids learn to do things by themselves within safe limits. For example, helping make part of their lunch teaches them to be more independent.
- **Trust and Consistency:** When rules are the same all the time, kids learn to trust their parents and to be reliable themselves. A rule like doing homework before TV helps them trust their daily routine and understand why it's important to do their work first.

How To Handle Disrespect

Do you wonder why your child is being rude and disrespectful to you or to others? Double check your own actions. Young kids learn how to act towards others, like their grandparents, by watching what their parents do, and they don't always understand that adults are different from them. So, if a child sees their parents not being nice to their grandparents, they might start acting the same way.

Additionally, since children don't always manage their emotions and moods well, a child may be grumpy or easily upset, causing them to be rude to others too.

What should you do? The most important thing is to let them know right away, in a calm manner, that it's not okay. If you ignore the behavior, they might think it's fine to be rude. On the other hand, if you shout or get really mad, it may make them more upset.

The best way is to be firm but kind. Tell them what they did wrong and show them the right way to behave. It's about helping them learn how to be nice, not just telling them off. Here are 4 steps to help handle a disrespectful child:

— Step 1: Immediate and Clear Correction

Imagine your child just acted rudely towards grandma. It's time to gently but firmly point out the mistake. Right away, let them know why it's wrong: "Talking rudely to grandma isn't respectful," or "We don't yell at grandma, it's unkind." It's crucial to explain clearly rather than just questioning or reprimanding them in a vague manner. However, if correcting them in front of grandparents could be embarrassing, take them aside privately to discuss the issue.

— Step 2: Show the Right Way

Children thrive on clarity. Instead of just saying "Be polite," demonstrate what that looks like: "Let's greet grandma with a warm hello and a smile." Keep instructions simple and relatable.

Additional Tip: To teach proper manners, you can play pretend games with your child. Act out situations where people greet each other politely, like saying hello and smiling. This way, your child can practice good manners in a fun and playful way.

— Step 3: The Dos and Don'ts List

Sit down with your child and create a list of positive behaviors (the Dos) and negative behaviors (the Don'ts). For the Don'ts, include actions like speaking rudely or not greeting elders. For the Dos, list respectful behaviors like using polite words and smiling. Place this list somewhere visible and go over it regularly. This isn't just about rules; it's a guide for respectful interactions, discussed and understood together.

Additional strategy for the Don'ts list: To address mocking or mimicking behavior, include, "Don't mockingly repeat what others say" as one of the behaviors to avoid.

— Step 4: Using Rewards and Consequences Wisely

Implement a system of rewards and consequences. If they follow the Dos, they get a positive marker like a sticker. Accumulating these can lead to a small reward. However, if they engage in Don'ts, use a suitable consequence, like a timeout from a favorite activity. This method teaches them the consequences of their actions in a fair and constructive manner.

Keep in mind that teaching your child respect won't happen quickly. It takes time, effort, and lots of deep breaths. But all of your hard work will pay off in the end.

Easy Practical Exercises for Teaching Respect

— Role-Playing Respect:

Pretend with your child. You can act as someone being rude, and they can be respectful. Discuss why being respectful is better. For example, act out a scenario where you try to grab at their toys and they show you how to share. Then reverse the roles.

— Daily Kindness Challenge:

Every day, ask your child to do one nice thing for someone. It could be as simple as helping set the table or saying or doing something nice. For example, "Let's help grandma carry her groceries."

— Empathy Stories:

Read stories or watch shows where characters have feelings. Talk about how those characters feel and why. For example, after watching a movie, discuss why the main character felt sad and how your child could help someone else in that situation.

Bad behaviors

As a parent, we should never ignore the following bad behaviors. Very bad behavior needs a response to reinforce that it's unacceptable. Here are some common behaviors and how to handle them:

— Taking things that aren't theirs

Imagine your child comes home with a toy that isn't theirs. It's like us borrowing a neighbor's lawn mower without asking – not good, right? Sit down with them, explain why it's important to respect other people's things, and guide them to return the toy and apologize. Maybe a timeout from their favorite game will help the lesson stick.

— Causing harm for attention

Kids can be little drama kings and queens, acting up to get our eyes on them. If your little one grabs a toy from a friend and causes a scene, it's time for a heart-to-heart talk. Help them understand how their actions affect others. A lesson in kindness and requiring a sincere apology to the friend can turn the situation around.

— Mocking difference

If your kiddo pokes fun at someone, it's time for a gentle but firm chat. Help them see that everyone is unique and special, and that's what makes the world an interesting place. Maybe share a story from your childhood about learning to appreciate differences. Have them apologize and find ways to be a friend instead.

— Leaving someone out

We all know being left out stings. If your child is not including a classmate, it's a chance to teach empathy. Talk to your child about how it feels to be left out and tell them they should never do that to anyone. Encourage them to include the child who is being left out in their play.

— Lashing Out in Anger

Kids are still *kids*, and they may still have trouble handling their emotions or controlling how they feel, just like adults do sometimes. However, some kids respond more strongly than others. For example, some kids will scream, hit people, and even break anything they can get their hands on just to be heard. If you notice such behavior, you need to work with your child.

Your reaction should be based on your child's age and how bad their behavior was. Once the storm has passed, chat about better ways to handle big feelings, like drawing or talking it out. Cleaning up together or fixing what was broken can be part of making amends.

Together With Grandparents

Picture yourself as the captain of a ship named *Parenting*, with grandparents as your co-captains. To successfully navigate the seas of discipline and manners, it's essential that everyone is sailing in the same direction.

Let's say grandma and grandpa are the cool type, shrugging off a bit of sass with a "Kids will be kids" attitude. Here's where a friendly family chat helps. Sit down with them and share your vision - a united front is crucial for teaching Junior about respect and manners. Sometimes, all it takes is a gentle nudge like, "Remember to greet grandma nicely," or a simple "Use kind words with grandpa," to reinforce those golden rules of politeness.

Now, reflect on your own behavior as parents. Kids are like little sponges – they soak up everything they see. Show them how it's done. A warm "Good morning" or a smile can go a long way in setting a positive example.

And who says learning manners can't be fun? Bring out those colorful picture books about good behavior, or have a little puppet show where Teddy learns to say "Please" and "Thank you." It's learning, disguised as playtime!

However, be mindful of your child's temperament. If your child is shy, gently encourage them without pushing too hard. Avoid physical reprimands and harsh scolding. It's about encouraging enforcement.

In this collaborative effort, the secret sauce is consistency, understanding, and a sprinkle of fun. By working together with grandparents and leading by example, you're setting your child on a path of respectful and kind behavior. Remember, raising a well-mannered child is a team effort, and each member plays a vital role in this beautiful journey.

Parenting Challenges

Scenario: 10-year-old Ethan comes home from school visibly upset. He slams the door and shouts about his day.

Typical Response:

Ethan: "I am tired of school. It's so stupid! I hate it!"

Parent: "Why did you slam the door? That won't solve anything. You're so bad-tempered."

Ethan: "You always shout at me! You're not helping!"

Result: The situation escalates, leaving both Ethan and the parent stressed. Ethan feels misunderstood and upset, while the parent feels disrespected and angry.

Improved Mindful Response:

— Step 1: Talk about the problem

Parent: "Ethan, **I noticed** you slammed the door and sounded upset about school. It's okay to feel frustrated, but slamming doors isn't the best way to handle it."

Ethan: "But today was just awful."

— Step 2: Explain what to do next time

Parent: "I understand you had a tough day. Why don't you sit down and tell me about it. (Allow Ethan to share his struggle before additional correction.)

Parent (after listening and when Ethan is calmer): **Next time** you're upset, remember to talk it out or take deep breaths instead of shouting or slamming doors. This way, you can express yourself more calmly. Does that sound like something you can do?"

Ethan: "I guess I can try that."

— Step 3: Discuss consequences

Parent: "If we continue with door-slamming and yelling, we might need to limit some privileges, like gaming. Remember, it's important to communicate in ways that draw people in, not push them away."

Ethan: "I don't want people to avoid me."

— Step 4: Confirm understanding

Parent: "Can you recap what we've discussed?"

Ethan: "When I'm upset, I should talk to you or breathe deeply instead of yelling or slamming doors. Continuing to do so might cost me my gaming time, and it could push people away."

Parent: "That's right. And remember, I'm here for you, no matter what."

Result: By addressing Ethan's emotions and providing constructive alternatives, the parent diffuses the situation, fostering cooperation and understanding.

Remember to approach disrespectful situations as learning opportunities. See the misbehavior as a chance to teach kids about respect and healthier ways to communicate.

Reaction Training

Scenario 1: Talking Back

Emma, a 9-year-old, often talks back disrespectfully, like responding with "Whatever" or rolling her eyes when asked to do something she doesn't want to.

Your Typical Reaction:

- You react with frustration: "Don't talk to me like that!"
- You attempt to lecture Emma about being disrespectful.
- Sometimes you ignore the behavior, uncertain of an effective response.

Your desired reaction using the 4-Step Mindful Response:

— Step 1: Talk about the problem

Parent calmly but firmly addresses the behavior: "Emma, I've noticed that you've been acting disrespectfully. Responding with "Whatever" or rolling your eyes is not okay."

— Step 2: Explain what to do next time

Parent: "I understand you might be upset or not want to do something, but next time you need to speak kindly. Let's try responding again, shall we?"

— Step 3: Discuss consequences

Parent: "If this disrespectful behavior continues, we might need to reconsider some of your privileges, like time with friends or using your phone. This isn't about punishment, but about learning to respect each other."

— Step 4: Confirm understanding

Parent: "Can you tell me our agreement about how we talk to each other? What happens if we forget?"

Emma: "I should talk nicely, even if I'm upset. If I keep being disrespectful, I might lose some privileges."

Parent: "Exactly. It can be hard, but respectful communication is important. Thank you for understanding, Emma."

Scenario 2: Refusal to Do Homework

Now it's your turn. Consider your typical reaction to the following scenario and record it below. Then think of a more mindful response and write it down.

10-year-old Mia pushes her homework aside, saying she'll do it later, and starts playing with her toys, ignoring your reminders.

Your Typical Reaction:

_____
_____
_____
_____
_____
_____

Your desired reaction using the 4-Step Mindful Response:

_____
_____
_____
_____
_____

"BEFORE YOU SPEAK IN
ANGER, REMEMBER THAT
YOUR WORDS CAN PLANT
GARDENS OR BURN WHOLE
FORESTS DOWN."
– ANONYMOUS

@NOYELLINGPARENTINGTOOLBOX

C H A P T E R 9

SIBLING RIVALRY

Remember those days? *"Stop fighting this instant!"* or *"I don't care who started it, you're both grounded!"* Ring any bells? These are the phrases many of us grew up hearing, the soundtrack of our own sibling rivalries. And now, as parents, we catch ourselves repeating these familiar lines, almost like we're stepping into our parents' shoes during those moments of chaos and noise.

Think about it – the way we were raised, the lessons soaked up from our own parents, they shape us in more ways than we realize, especially when it comes to mediating our children's squabbles. It's a bit like an old recipe handed down through generations. We find ourselves adding the same ingredients our parents did, often without thinking. When in reality, with all that we now know, the recipe needs to be updated, using the same love of course, just made a little healthier.

But here's a comforting thought: we have the power to add our own flavors to this recipe, to change the ingredients. This chapter is all about exploring that. It's a heart-to-heart on how our past influences our present and how we can gently shift towards a more understanding, nurturing way of handling those inevitable sibling tiffs.

Together, we'll unpack these memories, understand their impact, and learn new, loving ways to guide our kids through their disagreements. It's not just about keeping the peace; it's about a nurturing home where every squabble is a stepping stone to stronger sibling bonds and a deeper family connection. Let's turn those "Stop fighting!" moments into opportunities for growth and understanding.

Why Sibling Fights Happen

Have you ever wondered why brothers and sisters sometimes don't get along? It's a bit like when everyone wants to play with the same toy, but there's only one toy to go around.

- **The Battle for Attention:** In this classic scene, each child is trying to be the star of the family show, hoping to catch mom's or dad's eye. Sometimes, when one kiddo feels a bit left out, they might kick up a fuss just to get that spotlight back on them. It's like when everyone's trying to talk over each other at the dinner table – chaos!
- **The Comparison Game:** We have to be careful not to compare children since each one is unique. When we say things like, "Your brother's room is always so tidy, why isn't yours?"

we might not realize it, but we're setting the stage for a bit of a rivalry. You'll be unintentionally starting a competition where everyone feels they need to outdo the other to win your approval, or stirring up resentment in the child who feels like they can't measure up.

- **Chalk and Cheese Personalities:** Siblings can be as different as, well, chalk and cheese. One might love quiet time with a book, while the other's all about running wild outdoors. When their worlds collide, it's no surprise that sometimes they just don't get each other, leading to those "You're so weird!" moments.

- **The Sharing Saga:** Whether it's toys, the TV remote, or the last cookie, sharing can be tough. It's like when friends have to decide who gets to play with the new toy first – there's bound to be a bit of a tiff.

Understanding these little triggers helps us see the bigger picture. Sibling fights often stem from the hustle for attention, the pressures of comparison, personality clashes, and the age-old dilemma of sharing. With a bit of patience, we can help our little ones navigate these choppy waters, teaching them that, despite their differences, being siblings is pretty awesome.

Understanding Their Differences

Think of your family as a beautiful garden, where each kid is a unique flower, each with their own needs. Just like you wouldn't water a delicate orchid and a hardy cactus the same way, each child requires a special blend of care and attention based on their distinct personalities.

Being a parent means understanding that your approach to nurturing each child might differ, and that's perfectly okay. It's not about boxing them in, with labels like "oldest" or "youngest," but about recognizing their individuality.

The eldest, often burdened with expectations like "You're the big sister, set an example!" needs to be seen as a child too, not just a role model. They deserve to be heard and to sometimes shirk the mantle of responsibility.

And although the youngest might be the twinkling star of the home, they also need to learn self-reliance and responsibility. It's important not to always swoop in to solve their problems. Let them face some challenges; it's for their own growth.

Stepping back and viewing your children as individuals, not just a part of a birth order sequence, allows you to appreciate their unique viewpoints. This approach helps in reducing sibling rivalry and misunderstandings. However, handling each child differently can sometimes lead to accusations of unfairness. For example, if you let the younger one pick the movie, the older one might feel sidelined. Or incessant praise for the eldest can make the youngest feel overlooked. Remember, children have a keen sense of justice, and they quickly pick up on any perceived imbalance.

To manage this, base your decisions on their needs rather than an abstract sense of fairness. When they cry, "It's not fair!" gently explain, "Fair doesn't always mean equal. It means giving each of you what you need to thrive." In this nurturing environment, you'll cultivate a garden where every flower blooms beautifully.

When to Step In

In situations where siblings quarrel, it's best to let them sort it out themselves. Step in only if things might get rough. If you're always the referee, they won't learn to fix problems on their own. Plus, they might think you're picking favorites, which isn't cool. And the kid you always save? They might start thinking they can do anything and get away with it.

However, if they're saying mean things, it's totally fine to teach them nicer words to use. That's not the same as breaking up the fight.

If you do need to step in, here's what to do:

- Give them a break from each other. No need to go over the fight right then and there. Wait till everyone's chilled out.
- Don't play the blame game. It's not just about who started it, both are usually responsible.
- Find a win-win. For example, if they're both after the same toy, help them find a fun game they can play together.

Remember, this is how they learn how to see the other's point of view, how to compromise, and how to keep their cool.

Parent Hacks

Sibling rivalry shouldn't be new to you if you have more than one child. But here's the thing – regardless of how many conflicts you deal with, don't let it shake your confidence in parenting.

- **Toy Tussle**: When your kids are locked in a battle over a toy, the fight can escalate quickly. First, remove the toy in question from the scene and send a clear message: "Either you play nice, or you don't play at all!"

- **Sibling Showdown**: When your kids are raising their voices, and there's a wrestling match in your living room, it's time to step in. Separate them and have them go in different directions. This allows you to press a reset button on their emotions.

- **Remote Wars**: You should be familiar with the age-old battle for the television remote. Now is the time to bring a logical consequence: "If anyone fights, I am turning off the TV."

- **Timeouts**: You can use timeouts like a pit stop in a race. The idea is not to punish your kids but to ensure they take a breather to cool down and regroup.

- **Privileges and Responsibilities**: For the older kids, ensure you mix privileges with responsibilities. When they get the joy of staying up later, they should also be reminded of the responsibility of setting a good example. Always use the popular mantra for your kids, "With great power comes great responsibility."

- **Ignoring When Needed**: Introduce your older kids to strategic ignoring. Teach them that not every little poke or prod from their younger sibling deserves a reaction. They can easily shrug or walk away.

- **Discouraging Tattling**: Make tattling unrewarding by allowing your kids to work things out themselves, unless it's a matter of safety.

Sometimes, all kids need is to be seen and heard. Ensure you give each child some spotlight and let them enjoy it. This can be as simple as reading a book, taking a 10-minute walk, or watching a movie together. There'll be less bickering when they don't need to compete for your attention.

Parental Insights

When managing sibling rivalry, here's a mindset to adopt: friction between siblings is normal. So, instead of striving for a utopia where everyone gets along all the time, let's work toward having a home where conflicts are resolved healthily.

- **Expect sibling rivalry**: Sibling rivalry is natural; it's part of growing up. So don't fault your parenting skills if your kids go at each other, and don't expect that your home will *always* be calm.
- **Fairness over equality**: Explain to your kids that fairness isn't about everything being the same but everyone's needs being met in the best way possible.
- **Make every child feel special**: Acknowledge and celebrate your kids' unique qualities and achievements. Spend one-on-one time with them, showing interest in their hobbies and recognizing their strengths.
- **Avoid playing favorites**: Playing favorites can damage your child's self-esteem and relationships with each other. Instead, treat each child based on their needs and merits and avoid comparing them with their siblings.
- **Establish clear family rules**: Set clear expectations for behaviors that align with your family rules and enforce them consistently – for example, no hitting, name-calling, or foul language. When your kids know what to expect, they'll be more likely to cooperate.
- **Understand developmental stages**: Adjust your expectations to suit each child's age and developmental stage. For example, younger kids usually struggle with sharing; you should be patient and gradually teach them how to share.
- **Know when to step in**: If a situation gets out of hand, it's time to step in before someone gets hurt.

Your role as a parent is to calm your kids' storms. Be patient, consistent, and empathize; you're gradually helping them build a beautiful relationship that'll last a lifetime.

Parenting Challenges

Scenario: Sarah, 8, and Emily, 6, are in a heated argument over a toy. Both insist it's their turn to play, and the disagreement is quickly escalating.

Typical Response:

Parent: "Why can't you two get along?! Sarah, you're older and should know better!"

Sarah: "But she always gets her way because she's younger, and it's not fair!"

Parent: "That's not true. You're just upset."

Emily: "No, *she* always takes *my* toys, and no one stops her!"

Result: The tension increases, and the focus has shifted from the initial problem – sharing the toy – to a war over who is wrong, who gets favored, or who bears the labeling burden. As a result, there's sibling rivalry, and both children feel unheard and misunderstood.

Improved Mindful Response:

— Step 1: Talk about the problem

Parent: **"I see** we're having trouble sharing the toy and deciding whose turn it is."

Sarah: "But it's my turn now, Mom!"

Emily: "No way! She's been playing with it all morning!"

— Step 2: Explain what to do next time

Parent: "I understand both of you want a turn. Here's **what we're going to do next time**: Let's use 'rock-paper-scissors' to decide who plays first. Each of you can play for 10 minutes, then switch. Does that sound fair?"

Sarah: "That seems fair!"

Emily: "I like rock-paper-scissors! But what if she doesn't stick to the rules?"

— Step 3: Discuss consequences

Parent: "I trust you both to play fair. But if there's any cheating or fighting, the toy will be put away for the day. Can we agree on this way of sharing?"

Sarah & Emily: "Okay. We'll do 'rock-paper-scissors' and take turns."

— Step 4: Confirm understanding

Parent: "Let's make sure we all understand. Can you tell me what our plan is?"

Sarah & Emily: "Okay. "We play 'rock-paper-scissors' for the toy. If we fight or cheat, the toy gets put away for the day."

Parent: "That's great! I'm proud of how you both agreed to share and take turns."

Result: By using the No-Yelling-Formula, not only is peace restored to your living room, but your kids can now practice patience, problem-solving, and turn-taking.

Reaction Training

Scenario 1: Art Set Dispute

Lucy, 10, and Sarah, 8, keep fighting over who gets to use the new art set. They argue every day about it, and it's becoming a headache for everyone.

Your Typical Reaction:

- You try to be fair, saying things like, "Lucy, you had it yesterday, now it's Sarah's turn," but they still argue.
- Sometimes you just want to put the art set away to stop the arguing.

Your desired reaction using the 4-Step Mindful Response:

1. **Talk about the problem-** "Girls, I see you both love the art set, but this arguing has to stop. It's not fun for anyone when you fight like this."
2. **Explain what to do next time-** "Here's what we're going to do: you each get the art set for one hour after dinner. We'll set a timer. When your time is up, it's your sister's turn. No arguing."
3. **Discuss consequences -** "If this arguing keeps up, we'll have to put the art set away for a while. I don't want to do that, but we need peace at home."
4. **Confirm Understanding-** "So, what's our new rule about the art set?"

Lucy and Sarah: "We each get it for an hour. No fighting, or it gets put away."

Parent: "Exactly. Thanks, girls. I know you can do this."

Scenario 2- Sibling Sports Rivalry:

Emma, who is 10, and Noah, who is 8, both love playing soccer. At home, they often try to outdo each other, arguing about who is the better player. This competition causes a lot of arguments and hard feelings between them.

Think about your typical reaction and write it below. Then consider a more mindful response using the 4-Steps.

Your Typical Reaction:

_____

_____

_____

_____

_____

_____

_____

_____

Your desired reaction using the 4-Step Mindful Response:

_____

_____

_____

_____

_____

_____

_____

_____

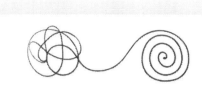

"A MOMENT OF PATIENCE
IN A MOMENT OF ANGER
SAVES A THOUSAND
MOMENTS OF REGRET."
– ANONYMOUS

@NOYELLINGPARENTINGTOOLBOX

C H A P T E R 10

TOO MUCH SCREEN TIME

In today's digital age, many of us have experienced moments when we've had to hand over our phones to our children to keep them occupied while we shop or have allowed YouTube to entertain them briefly. There's no judgment here – we've all been there. These quick fixes have become commonplace, but they come with their own set of challenges.

Frustration with our kids' screen time can quickly mount. The familiar cries of "How many times do I have to tell you to turn off that iPad?" or "That's it! No more games today!" might echo in your home. And who hasn't threatened to take away the phone after one too many episodes of *Cocomelon*?

If this sounds familiar, rest assured, you're not alone. However, before we rush to criticize all digital distractions, let's take a moment to acknowledge the benefits of some. They can be fantastic learning tools for kids. From creative online classes to educational apps, a world of knowledge is just a tap away for our children.

Nevertheless, the pressing question remains: How can we effectively manage screen time without it turning into a constant battle? How can we maintain peace at home without constantly playing the role of the screen police? This chapter provides the answers you need. It will help you find the balance without resorting to a complete ban. Let's explore practical solutions to help call a truce in screen-time battles.

Risks of Excessive Screen Time

These days, it's a common sight: kids as young as toddlers with tablets in hand, almost as if they were born with them. According to Common Sense Media, a large number of children under eight are now spending about two hours a day staring at screens. This surge in digital engagement among the very young has sparked a conversation about its potential impacts on their growth and development.

Dr. Jennifer F. Cross, associated with New York-Presbyterian Komansky Children's Hospital, echoes these concerns. She points out the emerging evidence of structural brain changes in children who spend significant time in front of screens. It's a delicate balance, she suggests, between harnessing the educational benefits of technology and ensuring that children also have ample time for play, exploration, and social interaction away from digital devices.

The key, as highlighted by experts and observers alike, is finding a middle path. While technology is undeniably a part of our lives, ensuring that children grow up with a healthy mix of screen time *and* real-world experiences is essential. After all, the world outside the screen offers invaluable lessons and adventures that are critical for a child's holistic development.

I've noticed it too, out and about, kids totally zoned into devices, oblivious to the bustling life around them. They don't get to chat with other kids, watch the dogs play in the park, or see moving trucks – important stuff that teaches them about the real world. Kids need to see, hear, and, most especially, interact with people to learn.

To kids, every single thing can be new and exciting. They have the urge to touch, see, smell, and hear the world around them so they can really understand it. This is how they learn. But if they are given unlimited access to screens, they'll be deprived of the following:

- **Physical and motor skills**: How can a child develop these skills if they're mostly sitting and watching? It's like learning about bike riding from a book but never actually getting on a bike.
- **Language and communication**: Watching cartoons and playing games don't foster interactive communication. There's no back-and-forth, no questions asked and answered. It's passive, not active learning.
- **Emotional intelligence:** When a child feels upset, instead of being taught how to manage their emotions, they get handed a tablet. This won't solve the root cause – it's like putting a band-aid on a splinter. It's a temporary fix, not a solution to understanding and dealing with feelings.

While screens do offer educational content, nothing beats hands-on, active learning. Kids need to run, jump, play, and explore. They need to practice speaking, listening, and interacting with others. Technology is a helpful tool, sure, but it shouldn't be the only resource in our parenting toolkit. Let's embrace it wisely, ensuring our kids get the best of both worlds – the digital and the real.

Evaluate Your Screen Time Practices

Before we dive into effective strategies for managing screen time, it's essential to assess your current practices. This self-assessment quiz will help you understand your kids' screen time habits better and identify areas for improvement.

Please answer the following questions honestly:

Question 1: On average, how many hours of screen time do your children engage in per day?

- Less than 1 hour
- 1-2 hours
- 2-3 hours
- 3-4 hours
- More than 4 hours

Question 2: Do you have specific rules or schedules in place for your children's screen time?

- Yes, we have clear rules and schedules.
- We have some guidelines, but they are not consistently followed.
- No, we do not have any rules or schedules in place.

Question 3: How often do you actively engage with your children during their screen time activities?

- Always, I regularly participate with them.
- Occasionally, when I have time.
- Rarely, I let them use screens independently.

Question 4: Have you noticed any negative effects of excessive screen time on your children, such as changes in behavior or sleep patterns?

- Yes, we have observed negative effects.
- We are unsure if screen time causes negative effects.
- No, we have not noticed any negative effects.

Question 5: Are there designated screen-free zones or times in your home?

- Yes, we have specific areas and times where screens are not allowed.
- We have some screen-free zones or times, but they are not consistently enforced.
- No, screens are accessible throughout our home at any time.

Question 6: How often do you discuss the importance of balanced screen time with your children?

- Frequently, we have regular conversations about it.
- Occasionally, but not as often as we should.
- Rarely, we have not discussed it with our children.

Question 7: Do you involve your children in non-screen-related activities, such as outdoor play, reading, or creative arts?

- Yes, we actively encourage and participate in non-screen activities.
- We encourage them, but they are more inclined toward screens.
- No, our children primarily engage in screen-related activities.

What Your Quiz Results Mean:

Let's look at your family's screen time and what changes could help.

- Mostly "Less than 1 hour" or "1-2 hours" picks: Great job! You're keeping screen time in check and mixing it up with other fun activities. Keep it going with lots of different experiences to help your child grow.
- Lots of "2-3 hours" and "3-4 hours" answers: You're in the middle. Yes, there are some rules, but there's room to cut back on screen time. Try adding more activities that don't involve screens to your child's day.
- Choosing "More than 4 hours" or "no real rules about screen time": Time for a change. Setting up some rules, like screen-free times or places, and getting your child involved in other activities can make a big difference.
- "Noticed negative effects from too much screen time or haven't talked about it much?": It's a good moment to get involved and talk about screen time. Try doing things together that don't involve screens and setting some guidelines to help balance out the day.

It's all about finding the right balance that works for your family, making sure screens are part of the fun but not taking over. Use these insights to guide you towards a more balanced digital life for your family.

Screen Time Smarts

You're probably no stranger to the scenario where kids test your screen time rules. They might throw tantrums or persistently ask you to change the rules just so they can have more screen time. So, how can you handle this situation effectively and maintain consistency in your screen time rules? Let's dive into some strategies.

- **Set clear screen time schedules:** Instead of vague timings, be precise. Say, "You have 30 minutes of screen time before dinner." This clear boundary makes it easier for your child to understand and for you to enforce. It's a balanced approach: your kids enjoy their screen time, and you get a predictable window to manage your own tasks.

- **Incentivize with screen time:** Use screen time as a carrot for positive behavior. Clearly outline what tasks or behaviors will unlock extra minutes of screen time. For instance, "Finish your homework by 5 p.m. and earn 15 extra minutes of screen time." To keep it engaging and clear, why not craft a "Screen Time Rewards" chart? It will be a fun, visual tracker for both you and your kids to monitor progress and rewards.

- **Define screen-free zones and times**: Be firm about where and when screens are a no-go. Bedrooms and dining tables should be screen-free zones. Also, carve out screen-free moments, like during family dinners or the hour before bedtime. This not only fosters better sleep routines but also strengthens family bonds.

- **Model healthy screen habits:** Remember, kids mimic what they see. If you're asking them to disconnect during meals, make sure you're setting the example. Putting your own devices away not only reinforces the rule but also opens up opportunities for more meaningful family time.

Remember, your rules don't need to be extreme. Ask yourself a few key questions to ensure they're balanced and effective:

- Does my child get enough sleep and eat healthily?
- Is my child physically active daily?
- Does my child maintain friendships and social connections?
- Are they spending quality time with the family?
- Is my child keeping up with schoolwork and homework?
- Do they engage in hobbies and activities they enjoy?

Your answer should guide you to make the right rules – not too strict, not too lenient. The idea is to maintain a balance.

Case Studies

- Smart Moves for Screen Time

— **Example 1:** Homework First, Play Later

Sarah had a simple rule for her son Jake: finish homework, then game time. She made sure his study spot was comfy and checked his work daily. Once done, Jake got 30 minutes of gaming. This neat trick turned homework into a breeze and gaming into a treat.

— **Example 2:** Story Time Beats Screen Time

David and Emily swapped Lily's late-night tablet scrolling with cozy bedtime stories. Lily picked the books, making it a fun ritual. This swap didn't just kindle Lily's love for stories; it also sent her off to dreamland, smiling and relaxed.

— **Example 3:** Mealtime is Family Time

Tom and Lisa kicked screens out of mealtime, making room for chitchats and giggles. They got everyone involved in cooking and setting the table, turning meals into a team effort. The result? Loads of laughter and heart-to-heart talks over yummy dishes.

— **Example 4:** Move More, Watch Less

John introduced a cool challenge for Emma: earn screen time by staying active. Whether it was biking, swimming, or helping around the house, every bit counted. They often teamed up, making it double the fun. This new game got Emma moving more and watching less.

— **Example 5:** Learn and Play

Amy turned Ben's screen time into a secret learning mission. She found cool apps that made math, science, and even coding super fun. They had a deal: learn something new, then discuss it together. Ben's screen time became a journey of fun discoveries!

Remember, every family is unique, and there's no one-size-fits-all solution when it comes to managing screen time. Feel free to tweak these strategies to fit your family's rhythm and routines. Being flexible and open to adapting these ideas can make your screen time journey even more effective and enjoyable. After all, finding the right balance is all about what works best for you and your kids.

Alternatives to Screen Time

There's a world of fun and learning experiences available for you and your kids outside screen time. Here are some alternatives:

- **Outdoor Fun:** How about trading screen time for green time? This can be as simple as a family hike, a bike ride, or a playful game of tag in the park. It's not just exercise; it's a bunch of laughs and a chance to explore the world around you together.

- **Arts and Crafts:** Set up a spot at home where you and the kids can get crafty. Try finger-painting, making collages, or building something out of clay. Just get creative and have a blast. You'll end up with some cool art and even cooler memories.

- **Reading and Storytelling:** How about a family trip to the library to pick out some exciting books? Or create your own story night at home, where everyone adds their part to a big family tale. It's a great way to let your imaginations run wild and have a good laugh together.

- **Games and Puzzles:** Break out the board games and puzzles for some classic fun. Whether it's racing to solve a puzzle or battling it out in Monopoly, these games are perfect for a little friendly competition and a lot of fun.

- **Cooking and Baking Together:** This is about way more than just making food – it's about the fun times you'll have together. Imagine your kids getting their hands into the dough or measuring out ingredients. Even toddlers can help chop veggies with toddler-safe knives you can find online. They'll be super excited to be involved and see what they can create. Your crew can make a simple sandwich, decorate cupcakes, or create a hearty and healthy soup. But these moments are about laughing, learning, and making some awesome memories together.

- **Gardening:** If you've got some outdoor space, why not start a small garden? Digging in the dirt, planting seeds, and watching them grow is not just cool – it's super satisfying, especially when you can eat what you've grown!

- **Helping Others:** Team up for some community service. It could be anything from helping at a local food bank to cleaning up a park. It's a great way to teach kids about giving back and working together for a good cause.

Each of these activities is a great way to have fun, learn, and make memories without screens. They're all about making the most of your time together and creating memories that'll last a lifetime.

Additional Resources

For further guidance on managing screen time and promoting healthy child development, consider exploring these valuable resources:

Book Recommendation: *The Tech-Wise Family: Everyday Steps for Putting Technology in Its Proper Place*, by Andy Crouch – This book provides practical insights and strategies for families to navigate the digital age wisely.

Website: Common Sense Media – Common Sense Media offers reviews and recommendations for age-appropriate movies, TV shows, games, and apps, helping parents make informed choices.

App: Screen Time Parental Control – This app allows parents to set screen time limits, track device usage, and ensure a healthy balance between screen time and other activities.

Book Recommendation: *Reset Your Child's Brain: A Four-Week Plan to End Meltdowns, Raise Grades, and Boost Social Skills by Reversing the Effects of Electronic Screen-Time*, by Victoria L. Dunckley, MD – Dr. Dunckley's book offers a comprehensive plan for resetting a child's brain from the effects of excessive screen time.

Website: Zero to Three – Zero to Three provides resources and information on early childhood development, including guidance on screen time for infants and toddlers.

App: Khan Academy Kids – Khan Academy Kids offers educational content for young children, promoting learning through interactive activities.

Book Recommendation: *The New Childhood: Raising Kids to Thrive in a Connected World*, by Jordan Shapiro – This book explores how digital technology can be integrated into children's lives for positive development.

Parenting Challenges

Scenario: Parent notices son, Max, spends many hours on his tablet daily. Out of frustration, the parent yells.

Typical Response:

Parent (frustrated): "You are always on that tablet! Can't you play outside for a change?!"

Max (upset): "Leave me alone!"

Parent (angered): "How dare you speak to me like that?!"

Result: The parent takes away the tablet forcefully, leaving Max feeling resentful and misunderstood.

Improved Mindful Response:

Parent observes that Max has been overusing screen time and approaches him calmly.

— Step 1: Talk about the problem

Parent (calmly): "Max, **I've noticed** you're spending a lot of time on your tablet lately. It worries me to see you glued to the screen so much."

Max: "But I like the games and videos."

— Step 2: Explain what to do next time

Parent: "I understand they're fun, but too much screen time isn't healthy for you. We need to cut down on it. **Next time** let's try an hour on weekdays after homework, and up to two hours on weekends. Does that sound reasonable?"

Max: "That's less than I want, but I guess."

— Step 3: Discuss consequences

Parent: "If you don't stick to these limits, we'll have to limit your tablet use further, or you could lose access to it for a while."

Max: "Alright, I'll watch the time."

— Step 4: Confirm understanding

Parent: "Can you tell me what we agreed on, just to make sure we're clear?"

Max: "I can use the tablet for one hour on weekdays after my homework is finished and two hours on weekends. If I go over, there might be more restrictions or a break from it."

Parent: "Right. I'm doing this because I care about you. We want you to enjoy your time both on and off the screen."

Reaction Training

Scenario 1: Challenges with Limiting Video Game Time

Oliver, 12, finds it hard to stop playing video games even after his allotted time ends. When told his gaming time is over, he often becomes moody and combative.

Your Typical Reaction:

- Telling Oliver "Gaming time is over," but he keeps playing, ignoring your words.
- Feeling frustrated: "You never listen, Oliver!"
- Eventually, you end up unplugging the console, leading to a meltdown and tears.

Your desired reaction in using the 4-Step Mindful Response:

— Step 1: Talk about the problem

Parent (calmly): "Oliver, I see you're having a great time with your game, but we agreed on a specific time for playing. Sticking to our schedule is important."

— Step 2: Explain what to do next time

Parent: "Remember, we agreed on one hour. Following this rule is important. Let's save your game and turn it off together."

— Step 3: Discuss consequences

Parent: "I know stopping can be hard, but if we can't stick to our agreement, I'll have to set a new rule where the console will be off-limits for a few days. It's not something I want to do, but it's important to keep our commitments."

— **Step 4: Confirm Understanding**

Parent: "Can you tell me how long your game time is supposed to be? And what will happen if you don't stick to it?"

Oliver: "I get to play for 1 hour, I won't be able to play at all for the next few days."

Parent: "Exactly, and I don't want to have to do that. Let's try our best to stick to the hour, okay?"

Scenario 2: Neglected Responsibilities

Emma, who is 10, constantly forgets to do her chores or homework because she's engrossed in watching YouTube videos or TikTok clips. Consider how you are prone to typically deal with the situation, then consider a more mindful response below.

Think about your typical reaction and write it below. Then consider a more mindful response using the 4-Steps.

Your Typical Reaction:

_____

_____

_____

_____

_____

_____

Your desired reaction using the 4-Step Mindful Response:

_____

_____

_____

_____

"YOUR CHILDREN WILL
FOLLOW YOUR EXAMPLE,
NOT YOUR ADVICE."
– ANONYMOUS

@NOYELLINGPARENTINGTOOLBOX

C H A P T E R 11

MEALTIME TANTRUMS

Now, let's get real about something that we've all experienced – mealtime tantrums. Picture this: you've lovingly prepared a meal and called your kids to the table, expecting a warm, family moment. But instead of joyful munching, you're greeted with whines and groans and the all-too-familiar chorus of "I'm not eating that!"

You may be wondering, "What do I do when my child throws a fit about coming to the table or refuses to eat what the rest of the family is having for dinner?" Though getting through dinner without tantrums may seem impossible, in this chapter, we will learn how to tackle those tantrums and how to navigate them without lashing out.

How Not To Yell

"Don't talk with your mouth full!" "Stop playing with your fork!" "Use your fork, not your hands!" "Don't drop that!" "Put it back!" "Why won't you listen?" Does this sound like a typical mealtime in your home? If these phrases are all too familiar, it might be time to reconsider how you're handling the small things at the dinner table.

Often, as parents, we can get caught up in the little things: sitting up straight, using utensils correctly, not fidgeting, cleaning up spills immediately, or those pesky crumbs on the floor. Sure, it's frustrating, but let's ask ourselves, do we really need to point out every single small thing during mealtime? It's crucial to learn to let the small things slide occasionally. Constantly getting worked up over minor issues can create a tense atmosphere and isn't usually effective.

Think about the last time you raised your voice over a pea rolling off the plate. Did it help? More often than not, it just leads to everyone getting upset, and it can end with the kids in tears. How you talk to your kids at mealtime really matters. A kinder, calmer voice can change the whole mood of dinner. It turns the table into a happy place, not a stressful one. This way, kids are more likely to listen and enjoy their meal, and you'll feel better too. Remember, a peaceful dinner is about more than just good food – it's about how we speak to each other.

Kids making a mess or being a bit unruly at the dinner table is normal. These behaviors often improve as they grow older. So, try to make mealtimes joyful and stress-free. If children look forward to sitting at the table with the family, the chances of mealtime meltdowns naturally decrease. It's about creating a happy, relaxed environment where everyone can enjoy their meal and each other's company.

Tips for Common Mealtime Meltdowns

Here are some common scenarios and tips for each one:

1. Refusal to Eat Certain Foods:

- Example: Your child avoids green vegetables like broccoli or spinach.
- Parenting Tip: Keep offering these vegetables, but without pressure. Serve broccoli as a side dish or mix spinach into a smoothie or pasta sauce. Consistency and patience are important. It often takes multiple exposures for a child to start trying new foods.

2. Demanding Only Specific Foods:

- Example: Your child wants to eat nothing but chicken nuggets every night.
- Parenting Tip: It's okay to start with their favorite foods, but try to introduce a new item alongside the familiar ones. For instance, if it's pasta with cheese, add a small portion of a new vegetable each time. Praise them when they try it, and be patient as their taste buds adjust.

3. Tantrums Over Touching Foods:

- Example: Your child gets upset if different foods on their plate touch each other.
- Parenting Tip: If your child is particular about foods touching, a divided plate can help. You can also involve them in setting up their plate, giving them a sense of control. Over time,

encourage them to try a little mixing, but respect their pace and preferences.

4. Fast Food vs. Home Meals:

- Example: Your child constantly asks for pizza instead of the meals you prepare.
- Parenting Tip: Involve your child in cooking simple, healthier versions of their fast-food favorites at home. This can be a fun activity and helps them appreciate the effort that goes into preparing meals. Plus, it gently nudges them towards healthier eating habits.

5. Mealtime Becomes Meltdown Time:

- Example: Your child often becomes tearful or angry during meals, refusing to eat.
- Parenting Tip: If emotions run high during meals, try to understand the underlying issues. Ensure there's a calm transition into mealtime, perhaps with a quiet activity beforehand. Address their concerns or frustrations separately from mealtime to avoid associating eating with stress.

6. Resisting the Mealtime Routine:

- Example: Your child prefers grazing throughout the day to sitting down for a full meal.
- Parenting Tip: If your child resists sitting down for meals, try to make mealtime more engaging. Have them help with simple tasks like setting the table or choosing what's for dinner. Consistent snack times and meals where everyone sits down together can also help establish a routine they'll grow to expect and enjoy.

How to Prevent Mealtime Tantrums

We can all agree that mealtime tantrums can be hard to navigate. So, let's talk about strategies to decrease them and make mealtimes a little less chaotic and a lot more fun.

1. Stick to a Routine

Kids thrive on routine. When dinner is at the same time each day, they know what to expect. A surprise schedule change can be as jarring for them as it would be for you if your work lunch was canceled just as you arrived at the restaurant. And while they do need to learn to be flexible, things will go smoother if you can stick to a routine as often as possible.

2. Heads-Up Helps

Imagine how you'd feel if you were engrossed in the final episode of your favorite Netflix drama, on the edge of your seat, when, out of nowhere, your partner switches off the TV. That's how kids feel when yanked away from playtime for dinner. A five-minute warning is like your partner giving you a gentle nudge, saying, "Hey, the final scene is wrapping up. Dinner in five?" It gives you time to mentally prepare for *your* next scene – mealtime. So, give your child a heads-up to prepare them for dinner by saying, " You have 10 more minutes to play" or "Food will be ready in 5 minutes."

3. No Pressure, Please

Don't force kids to eat or beg them to try just one more bite. This can make mealtime feel like pressure, not fun. Instead, make eating together a happy time that everyone will enjoy.

If your child is taking too long to eat or pushing his food around the plate, they're either not hungry, or perhaps don't like the food. It's better not to make eating feel like a big problem. Say things like, "It's okay if you don't love this food. Maybe we can eat something you like tomorrow."

Also, don't let kids have too many snacks before dinner. This way, they'll be hungry and ready to eat when it's time. If a child doesn't eat much at dinner and gets hungry before bed, it's okay to give them something small and healthy like a banana, apple, or carrot quickly before brushing their teeth. Point out that it's better for them to eat dinner with the family so they won't be hungry when it's time to go to sleep. This helps them learn to join in at mealtimes but still keeps them from going to bed hungry.

4. Choices, Choices!

Just like adults, kids enjoy having options. Asking, "Would you prefer apple slices or carrot sticks?" gives them a sense of control and helps to develop a positive sense of autonomy. Additionally, allowing them to choose what's for dinner once or twice per week will give them a voice and involve them in the process of mealtime. If they're having their pick of meals, they're more likely to gobble up the food.

5. Make mealtimes fun

Who says dinner has to be all "sit up straight and eat"? We need to relax and add a bit of fun to mealtime. Let's make it more like a mini-party. Though kids don't need to be wild at the dinner table, if someone drops food or spills a drink, don't make a big fuss. Forget the lectures and focus on enjoying the food and each other's company. Ask your kids playful questions about their meal, turning every bite into a little adventure. Ask about their day or what was on their favorite show during TV time. Keep things light and positive – no scolding, just smiles. This way, dinner becomes a time everyone looks forward to, filled with good food and even better vibes. Remember, the goal is happy, stress-free meals, not perfect table manners.

Parenting Challenges

Scenario: During dinner, Emma goes into tantrum mode by throwing her food on the floor. The parent becomes frustrated and starts to yell.

Typical Response:

Parent: "Why do you always act this way?! You don't behave well during meals. I'm tired of this happening all the time!"

Emma: "But I don't want to eat. Why are you making me?"

Parent: "Be quiet! Go to your room NOW!"

Emma is sent to her room without dinner, leaving her upset and confused.

Improved Mindful Response:

— Step 1: Talk about the problem

Parent: "Emma, **I see** that you're throwing your food on the floor during dinner. That's not how we behave when we eat, and it makes me sad to see food wasted."

Emma: "I didn't want to eat the food. I don't like it!"

— Step 2: Explain what to do next time

Parent: "I understand you might not always like what's on your plate, but instead of throwing it, you can tell me calmly, 'I'm not sure about this food,' and we can talk about it or find something else you'd prefer. Can you try that **next time**?"

Emma: "Yes, I can try that."

— Step 3: Discuss consequences

Parent: "If you keep having tantrums or throwing food, you will lose a privilege, like your bedtime treats. It's important to appreciate the food we have and avoid wasting it. We want dinner to be a pleasant time for everyone. Do you understand?"

Emma: "I don't want to miss treats."

— Step 4: Confirm understanding

Parent: "Great, Emma! To make sure you've got it, can you tell me what we just talked about?"

Emma: "If I don't want to eat something, I should say it calmly, not throw food. If I act out again, I will not get treats before bed. And I should be thankful for my food."

Parent: "That's right, Emma. I'm glad you understand."

Remember, some days will be smoother than others, which is totally fine. The goal is to create a positive environment where eating isn't a chore but an act that nourishes the body and enriches family bonds.

Reaction Training

Scenario 1: Spaghetti Squabble

Four-year-old Ethan often throws tantrums during dinner when spaghetti is served. He refuses to eat it and demands chicken nuggets instead.

Your Typical Reaction:

- Repeatedly trying to convince Ethan to eat his spaghetti, which often escalates the tantrum.
- Feeling frustrated and saying, "Ethan, you need to eat your spaghetti. It's what we have for dinner!"
- Eventually giving in and serving chicken nuggets to avoid a meltdown.

Your desired reaction with the 4-Step Mindful Response:

— Step 1: Talk About the problem

Parent (calmly): "Ethan, I notice you're not too happy about having spaghetti tonight. It's okay to prefer some foods over others."

— Step 2: Explain what to do next time

Parent: "But it's important we try what's served during dinner. It helps us enjoy different foods and stay healthy. Next time, let's take a small bite before we decide if we like it or not."

— Step 3: Discuss consequences

Parent: "If we keep getting upset over meals, we will have to miss out on dessert. I believe you can give the spaghetti a try without getting too upset."

— **Step 4: Confirm understanding**

Parent: "Can we go over our dinner rule? And what happens if we have trouble at mealtime?"

Ethan: "Try to eat what's on the plate, and if I make a big fuss, no dessert later."

Parent: "Exactly, Ethan. Let's try our best with the spaghetti, you might just like it!"

Scenario 2: Throwing Utensils or Food

When frustrated, Lucas, who is 5, sometimes tosses his fork or even throws food across the table. Analyze your typical reaction and record it below. Next, consider a more mindful response using the four steps demonstrated above.

Your Typical Reaction:

_____

_____

_____

_____

_____

_____

_____

Your desired reaction using the 4-Step Mindful Response:

_____

_____

_____

_____

_____

_____

"REMEMBER, YOUR VOICE
BECOMES YOUR CHILD'S
INNER VOICE; CHOOSE
WORDS THAT GUIDE, NOT
WORDS THAT WOUND."
– ANONYMOUS

@NOYELLINGPARENTINGTOOLBOX

C H A P T E R 12

BEDTIME BATTLES

Bedtime, that magical moment when the day is supposed to end peacefully, often turns into a wild adventure for parents. Many parents face bedtime battles with their kids, a common issue highlighted by child sleep experts and pediatricians. If just thinking about bedtime stresses you out, don't worry, you're not alone. Bedtime can be tough. I've been there too.

Here's a bit of my story. My challenge was getting my son to sleep by himself. My husband and I both worked long hours, but my son clung to me like a koala at bedtime. Picture this: it's late, we're both tired, and he insists on my company to fall asleep. The frustration was real.

You probably have your own bedtime sagas. Maybe your little one has turned into a bedtime ninja, sneaking out of bed when you're not looking. Or perhaps bedtime has become a negotiation table with a million questions or requests. If you're fed up with these bedtime battles, don't worry. This chapter will give you tools to make bedtime a breeze.

Why Bedtime Battle is Happening

Every parent knows, bedtime can sometimes feel like a showdown. But remember, there's always a reason behind your child's actions. The bedtime struggle could be due to sleep issues, behavioral aspects, or a mix of both. Let's dive into the potential reasons to shed some light on what's happening when it's time to hit the hay.

— Overtiredness:

Have you ever seen your kid bouncing off the walls at bedtime and thought, "Is this what a double espresso feels like?" As it turns out, when kids are super tired, they don't always conk out – sometimes, they go into overdrive. Their little bodies react by producing adrenaline, making them seem more wired than tired.

— Nap Time Overload:

Just like us, if kids catch Zs too late in the day, bedtime becomes a battle. That late nap might leave them too rested, making 7:00 p.m. feel more like the middle of the afternoon than bedtime.

— Bedtime Resistance:

We can't deny it – for kids, playing is more fun than sleeping. They see bedtime as an end to their fun, so they do all they can to resist it. Also, some kids fear the dark or sleeping alone, making bedtime even less appealing.

— Sleep Props:

Sleep props are things your kids need or depend on to fall asleep. Kids, like the rest of us, can get hooked on certain sleep rituals. Be it a pacifier, a favorite blanket, or even car rides, these sleep aids can be a big help. But reliance on them can make it tough for kids to nod off without their usual setup.

— Craving Connection:

Recognizing the need for connection is a game changer in your relationship with your child. Just like with my son, who resisted going to bed on time just to spend more time with me after a long day at daycare, it's a child's way of saying, "Stay a little longer; let's connect." The aim isn't to delay bedtime but to reach out for that deep, comforting connection they've missed all day. See it as an invitation to pause, understand your child's world, and respond with love and the presence they crave.

Create a Wind Down

After dinner, does your house buzz with the whirlwind of the evening? Dishes piling up, to-do lists for tomorrow, and maybe the kids glued to the screen while you juggle the chaos. You're on a mental sprint – lunches to prep, baths to give, teeth to brush. Everything's a race against the clock, and before you know it, you're herding the kids to bed at breakneck speed. But then, they're wide awake, and you're left wondering, "Why aren't they as tired as I am?" You might be tempted to insist, "Go to sleep, now!" But deep down, you know it's not that simple.

We're all swamped, especially when both parents are working full-time. But nobody wants that nightly battle of wills, that cycle of stress repeating itself. It's time for a shift.

So, take a moment. When your kids are bouncing off the walls at bedtime, pause and scan the scene. Is the room too bright? Is the TV still chattering away? Are toys and snacks scattered around, and have the bedtime rituals like a warm bath or toothbrushing been checked off?

Instead of getting frustrated with your little night owls, think about setting the stage for slumber. A peaceful bedtime isn't about demanding "lights out." It's about crafting a haven that whispers, "It's time to wind down." A dimmed room, a quiet backdrop, and a calm routine can make all the difference. Remember, it's not about hurrying up to sleep; it's about easing into it. Let's change the bedtime hustle into a bedtime harmony.

What Kids Want

Although we've briefly touched on the need for connection right before bed, it's worth mentioning here that connections are like your parenting superpower. Your kids are more receptive and cooperative when they feel connected to you. It's not just about getting them to follow instructions; it's about filling their emotional cup, making them feel seen and valued.

1. Quality Time

Children often cherish the simple moments spent with their parents. It's not the quantity of time that matters, but the quality. You don't need hours; even 5-10 minutes of focused quality time can make a big difference. Whether it's a quick game of hide and seek, a round of rock-paper-scissors, or any simple play, these moments matter. Being present means more than just being in the same room – it means being there with your heart and mind. Try carving out a story time each night or a weekly family game night. These are the moments that children remember and treasure, the ones that show them they're truly important in your life.

2. Hear Them Out

As adults, it's tempting to cut short our kids' stories with our "experienced" advice. We think we know better because we've been there. But remember, kids cherish being heard. They want to express themselves without immediate solutions being offered. So, next time, just listen. Let them rant, vent, and unload their feelings. Your patience in listening can build a foundation of trust and understanding for the future.

3. The Power of Praise

Your words carry weight. Instead of a generic "well done," get specific. Notice their efforts and comment on them. If your little one sorts their toys, try saying, "You're so organized! Thanks for making our home tidy." Or if they share with a friend, point out, "That was really kind of you to share your toys. You're a great friend." These moments of recognition are like sunshine for their self-esteem, nurturing a happy, confident child.

These small but meaningful gestures of appreciation boost their self-esteem and create a positive atmosphere at home. Your kind words become the building blocks of their confidence and happiness.

Remember, it's not about the quantity of time but the quality of your presence and the warmth of your words that matter most.

Peaceful Sleep Routines

Continuing from the idea of shaping a sleep-friendly environment, it's time to delve into the peaceful bedtime routine. Imagine those nights when your little ones slip into dreamland effortlessly, leaving you with a slice of serene "me" time. It may sound like a storybook ending for some, but it's within reach for all.

Crafting a peaceful bedtime isn't just a wish upon a star – it's an art and a science combined. The hustle and bustle of the day can transition into a tranquil night with the right touches. Here's how to make that peaceful bedtime routine not just a dream, but your family's reality:

— Start with a snuggle session

Set the stage for a peaceful night with a comforting "cuddle ritual." This cozy routine could include activities like reading a beloved book, giving a gentle massage, or playing tranquil music. These soothing activities are your gentle signal that bedtime is near. It's about wrapping up the day in a blanket of love and calm, readying your child for a night of sweet dreams.

— Find your daily rhythm

All families are unique. If you're the type that returns late from work, a 7 p.m. bedtime may not be realistic. It's okay to change the timetable to match your needs. However, consistency is key. Even if your children's bedtime is later, make it the same every night. Once they adapt to that schedule, they'll know what to expect and it will be easier for them to be prepared.

— Listen and validate feelings

Kids may delay going to bed because they have something in their thoughts. It could be school worries or a little spat with a friend. Take a moment to really listen. In these quiet minutes, you're not just a parent; you're a safe space for their thoughts and fears. When they feel heard, their brains relax, making it simpler to fall asleep.

— Stay as boring as possible

When bedtime comes, it's time to switch from Fun, Playful Parent to Night Parent. This might sound tough, but it's really important for helping your child go to sleep. Once you've said goodnight, try to be as calm and simple as you can. If you need to take your child back to bed again, just say something like, "Love you, time for bed."

Try not to make much eye contact and keep your face calm. Giving too much attention, even if it's just talking or looking, can make your child want to stay up longer. Don't worry, this won't last forever. Soon, your child will get used to this and bedtime will become easier for everyone.

A few small changes can turn bedtime from a hassle into something special. It's not about perfection, but about ending the day with peace and love. With a sprinkle of patience and a whole lot of heart, those bedtime struggles can turn into peaceful, starry nights with sweet dreams.

Parenting Challenges

Scenario: Four-year-old Mia has refused to go to bed. She started crying loudly, and the parent shouted in response to her misbehavior.

Typical Response:

Parent: "Enough already! Every night it's the same drama! Go to bed NOW!"

Mia: "You always yell at me. You never play. I hate this!"

Parent: "Your behavior makes me mad! You're acting spoiled. I can't deal with this!"

This reaction will only intensify Mia's cries and make bedtime more challenging.

Improved Mindful Response:

Facing Mia's bedtime resistance, the parent adopts a calm approach with the No-Yelling Formula.

— Step 1: Talk about the problem

Parent: "**I see** bedtime has been really tough lately, with a lot of crying and not wanting to go to bed. If you're not sleepy, crying loudly isn't the way to go. Let's find a better way, okay?"

Mia: "But I'm not tired. I don't wanna sleep yet."

— Step 2: Explain what to do next time

Parent: "I understand, sweetie. So, if you're not feeling sleepy, **let's try a different approach**. Instead of crying, let's talk about it calmly. Maybe a short story time before bed could help. What do you think?"

Mia: "Can I read for a bit, then?"

— Step 3: Discuss consequences

Parent: "Absolutely, a little reading time is fine. But remember, if bedtime turns into a big fuss, we might have to start the bedtime routine earlier to make sure you're getting enough sleep. We don't want you to be tired and grumpy in the morning, right?"

Mia: "No, I don't wanna be grumpy."

— Step 4: Confirm understanding

Parent: "Perfect. Now, just to make sure we're on the same track, what's our bedtime agreement?"

Mia: "If I'm not ready to sleep, I'll ask nicely instead of crying. If I fuss, bedtime is earlier. I need sleep so I'm not grumpy."

Parent: "That's right, Mia! A good night's sleep is important for all of us."

Of course, there'll be nights when things don't go according to the plan – the odd request for a glass of water, the occasional tantrums, and those times when things can't seem to settle. But with what we've discussed in this chapter, you're better equipped to handle bedtime tantrums.

Reaction Training

Scenario 1: Fear of Being Alone

Every time Nathan is put to bed, he expresses fear of monsters or shadows in his room, leading to the need for a parent to stay with him until he falls asleep.

Your Typical Reaction:

- Reassuring Nathan repeatedly that there are no monsters, which doesn't seem to ease his fear.
- Feeling exhausted and saying, "Nathan, there's nothing to be afraid of. You need to sleep in your own bed!"
- Eventually staying with him until he falls asleep to prevent an upset.

Your desired reaction using the 4-Step Mindful Approach:

1. Talk about the problem

Parent: "Nathan, **I see** you're really scared of monsters and shadows in your room. It's okay to feel scared sometimes."

2. Explain what to do next time

Parent: "But remember, our house is safe and those monsters are just in stories. **Next time** you feel scared, try hugging your teddy bear and remember it's there to protect you. We can also check for monsters together before bedtime to make sure they're all gone."

3. Discuss consequences

Parent: "If we spend too much time worrying about monsters, we might not have enough time for our bedtime story. It's important to trust that your room is a safe place so you can get a good night's sleep and be ready for fun tomorrow."

4. Confirm understanding

Parent: "Can you tell me what we can do if you're scared of monsters at bedtime?"

Nathan: "Check the room for monsters with you, hug my teddy bear, and try to sleep. If I still get scared and can't sleep, we might skip the bedtime story."

Parent: "Exactly, Nathan. Remember, your room is safe, and you're a brave boy. Let's give it a try tonight, and I bet you'll have sweet dreams!"

Scenario 2: Sleep Regression

Two-year-old Leo used to sleep through the night, but now he's suddenly waking up multiple times, crying or wanting to play. Think about what your typical reaction would be and write it below. Then consider what would be a more mindful approach using the 4 steps listed above.

Your Typical Reaction:

_____

_____

_____

_____

Your desired reaction using the 4-Step Mindful Response:

_____

_____

_____

_____

PART 4

FINAL THOUGHTS

As we reach the last part of this book, it's time to reflect on our journey so far. This isn't an end but the beginning of better ways of handling our emotions, interacting with our kids, understanding them, and growing alongside them more peacefully.

We can't deny it; parenting is an ever-evolving journey with challenges and successes. It's a path best paved with unconditional love, patience, and everyday learning. Yes, we've explored various tools and strategies, but know that the true essence of parenting is in the unique bond we share with our kids. Remember, parenting isn't one-size-fits-all. Our kids are unique, and what works for one may not work for another. Let's learn to listen more, adapt, and be present to decode their messages and respond calmly.

"UNCONDITIONAL LOVE IS LOVING
YOUR KIDS FOR WHO THEY ARE, NOT
FOR WHAT THEY DO... IT ISN'T
SOMETHING YOU WILL ACHIEVE
EVERY MINUTE OF EVERY DAY. BUT
IT IS THE THOUGHT WE MUST HOLD
IN OUR HEARTS EVERY DAY."
– STEPHANIE MARSTON

@NOYELLINGPARENTINGTOOLBOX

C H A P T E R 13

LOVE YOUR CHILD

L et's think about what it really means to love your child. It's not just about big hugs and I love yous. It's about understanding the little things they do and why they do them. In this chapter, we're going to get into the nitty-gritty of this. Loving our kids is about more than just the warm fuzzies; it's about really *getting* them, but also looking after ourselves, so we can be there for them.

All Behavior Is Communication

Have you ever heard or read somewhere that behavior is communication? One important thing we should never forget is that every little thing our kids do is their way of talking to us. When we look deeper and realize this, we'll suddenly see their giggles, tantrums, tears, and gazes make more sense.

Imagine Max, your little builder, passionately constructing a towering block castle. But in a flash, it collapses. Max's reaction? He gives those blocks a big kick. Old-school methods might call for a time-out, but let's spin this differently. Max's kick isn't just naughtiness. It's his way of saying, "This is so frustrating!" He doesn't have the words to express, "I'm upset because this is hard!"

When Max hits meltdown mode, instead of losing your cool, take a moment. This is your golden opportunity to teach him healthier ways to handle setbacks. Do you want a repeat of block-kicking next time? No way. You're guiding him to manage his feelings better. This isn't a moment for punishment, but for teaching resilience and expressing emotions in words.

Now, picture dinner time with Emma and her standoff with peas. The old script might call for an "eat your peas or else" approach. But let's reconsider. This isn't about forcing peas down; it's a chance for some genuine food talk.

Turn it into a game. Have Emma try a pea and then rate the taste, maybe on a scale from one to ten. It's a fun, no-pressure way to interact with her food. Or, get her hands-on in the kitchen. Kids who cook are often eager to try their culinary creations. This is less about eating peas and more about learning, exploring, and understanding food.

The *No Yelling Parenting Toolbox* is all about seeing these everyday moments not as battles, but as opportunities to connect and teach. It's about shifting from "Because I said so" to "Let's figure this out together." Every tantrum, stubborn refusal, or pushback is a step towards mutual understanding and growth. It's about seeing things from their little world's perspective. They're not just being difficult; they're communicating in their own way.

When we start seeing our child's behavior as communication, our approach to parenting will change. We'll move from trying to control their behavior to getting to the root of what our kids need and feel. With this knowledge, you aren't just sorting out the issue but laying down a rock-solid foundation of trust and understanding.

Don't Take It Personally

Parenting is tough, no doubt about it. There are days when everything seems to turn into a big deal for your kid, like when they decide broccoli is the worst thing ever. It's easy to start questioning yourself or your parenting during these tough moments, wondering why your child can't be calm like the neighbor's kid. Perhaps you find yourself frantically typing questions into Google, scouring articles about picky eaters, or scrolling through YouTube and Instagram in search of parenting advice.

But here's the thing: it's not about you or your parenting skills. Kids are just being kids. When Sam decides he's not into veggies, he's not saying you're a bad cook. He's just figuring out what he likes and doesn't like.

So, when things get heated and Sam says something mean, remember, he's not trying to upset you. He's just trying to express how he's feeling. It's your chance to teach him the right way to talk, even when he's mad. You can say, "I know you're mad, but we don't call each other names. We can talk about what's bothering you instead."

And if Sam's not excited about going to school, it's okay. Show him you understand and make a deal, like, "I know you'd rather stay home today. How about we plan something fun for after school?"

Remember, your child's behavior isn't a report card on your parenting. It's just part of growing up. By staying calm and showing you understand, you're teaching your child how to handle tough feelings and situations. Every hard moment is a chance to help your child learn and grow, and it's a chance for you to grow too. You're doing great as a parent, so don't take it personally.

Focus On Yourself

Let's talk about a super important, often missed piece of the parenting puzzle: **taking care of you**. That's right, you're more than just Mom or Dad. You're a person who needs some TLC too!

Ever had one of those mornings where you're running on zero sleep? You know, when the coffee doesn't hit, and everything feels like an uphill battle. Your kiddo spills their cereal, and instead of shrugging it off, you're ready to pull your hair out. It's because running on empty makes everything, including parenting, feel like a mammoth task.

Now, picture a different morning. You've kicked it off with some stretching or a quick jog. You're feeling like a superhero. That cereal gets spilled again, but this time, you're all smiles, cleaning it up while doing a little dance. What changed? You took a bit of time to charge up your batteries.

Mental health check: If you find yourself scrolling through social media and feeling down because everyone else seems to have it all together, hit that pause button. Remember, social media is like looking at life with rose-colored glasses – everything *seems* perfect, but it's not actually the full picture. Instead, find stuff that really makes you happy and fulfilled, not just stuff that looks good on a screen.

Let's redefine bedtime routines, focusing on yours, not just the children's. This isn't about avoiding the all-too-common Netflix binge (though saving that for a special weekend activity can indeed turn an ordinary night into a mini-event). It's about crafting a bedtime ritual that soothes the mind and prepares the body for rest, offering a unique twist to the everyday.

Consider starting with something unconventional yet simple: *a gratitude jar*. Spend a few minutes each night writing down one or two things you're grateful for on small pieces of paper and drop them into the jar. This practice not only shifts your focus from daily stresses but also sets a positive tone for the following day.

Next, integrate a bit of *aroma relaxation*. Essential oils like lavender or chamomile can be calming and are a simple, effective way to signal to your body that it's time to wind down. A few drops in a diffuser or on your pillow can make all the difference.

How about a *moonlight meditation*? If the weather permits, spend a few minutes outside under the night sky. This connection with nature can be incredibly grounding and a serene way to end the day.

Lastly, create a *nightly novel nook* – a cozy corner dedicated to evening reading. Switching from screen time to story time with a physical book can significantly improve your ability to fall asleep. Choose light, uplifting genres that steer your mind away from the day's worries.

Implement these steps, not necessarily every night, but perhaps once or twice a week to start. They're designed not just for better sleep but for a more peaceful, mindful end to your day. This approach offers a fresh take on the nightly routine, making it something you can look forward to rather than a chore.

In a nutshell, focusing on yourself is all about making sure you're not just surviving, but thriving. When you're feeling good, you're a super-parent, ready to take on anything from tantrums to teddy bear tea parties with a smile. Taking care of yourself isn't just good for you; it's great for your whole family. So if you want to be a happy, healthy parent, and equally have a happy, healthy home, remember to put yourself on the to-do list.

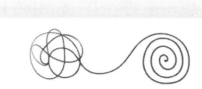

"IT'S NOT ABOUT BEING THE
PERFECT PARENT, IT'S ABOUT
BEING A PRESENT AND
COMPASSIONATE ONE."
– ANONYMOUS

@NOYELLINGPARENTINGTOOLBOX

C H A P T E R 14

HAPPY TOGETHER

The phrase "happy together" instantly warms the heart, doesn't it? It's about those simple, heartfelt moments. Like how 4-year-old Jack rushes to give you the biggest hug the moment you step through the door, or when 7-year-old Mia gazes up with those big eyes and whispers, "You're the best mom," making your heart skip a beat. And don't forget 12-year-old Jackson, who hands you a homemade birthday card, each handwritten word filling you with pride and joy. These moments might not make the evening news, but they're the golden ones, the memories that linger long after the day is done.

Yet, let's face it, parenting is not all sunshine and rainbows. One moment everything's picture-perfect, but the next, you're in the thick of childhood challenges, weathering the storm of a tantrum. It's in these tougher times that you realize parenting is as much about guiding yourself as it is about guiding your kids. It's about managing your expectations and your reactions. Through every giggle and every tear, we learn, we adapt, we grow. Because what we're really nurturing here isn't just a family; it's a journey of being happy together, turning everyday life into a symphony of love, understanding, and joy.

Positive Change

Imagine your family life as a cozy, sunlit garden, a place where things grow at their own pace, where care and patience are the order of the day. Just like a garden doesn't burst into bloom overnight, building a warm, loving family life is a journey, a series of small, thoughtful steps. We've all had those moments when our voice rises a bit too quickly, when frustration bubbles up faster than understanding. We're human; it happens. But just like pouring too much water can drown tender plants, sharp words can dampen a child's spirit.

Here's a comforting thought though: positive change is not only possible, it's within our reach, like the promise of spring after a long winter. It's about nurturing our family garden with intention and love. We don't simply scatter seeds of patience and hope for the best. We tend to them, we nourish them, we give them the warmth they need to flourish. This is the essence of our journey as parents. Every small act, every gentle word lays the foundation for something beautiful to grow.

So, when those challenging moments arise – and they will – let's try to see them in a new light. Instead of a sigh of, "Oh no, not this again," let's embrace a curious, learning mindset that asks, "Okay, what's this moment teaching us?" Every spilled drink, every untimely outburst isn't just a mess or a disturbance. It's an invitation to teach, to understand, and to grow, together, as a family.

Words are like sunlight and water to our family garden. They can nourish and they can wither. Instead of commands or quick reactions, let's lean into curiosity and warmth. Talk to your kids as if they're the most intriguing, delightful people you've met – because they are. Ask them questions, listen with your whole heart, and choose words that say, "I'm here with you, fully, in this moment."

Understanding our kids is a gentle art. Sometimes, we might see their actions through our grown-up lenses and miss the heart of their message. Remember, kids aren't just mini versions of adults. They have their own way of looking at the world, their own unique lenses. So let's pause, truly listen, and try to understand their perspective. Maybe that little tantrum is more about needing a nap or a reassuring hug than about the toppled blocks or the broken crayon.

Today, let's sow seeds of patience, empathy, and kindness. Every word of encouragement, every calm, attentive moment, every effort to see the world through our children's eyes all add to the richness of our family garden. This journey of changing how we react to our children isn't just about making our day smoother; it's about nurturing a family life where love, understanding, and mutual respect are in full bloom. Together, one small step, one seed at a time, we can turn our family garden into a thriving, joyful space of shared growth and warmth.

Visualize Your Day

Each morning, before the day gets busy, I take a short moment to picture a peaceful, happy day with my child. This isn't just planning; it's starting the day with love and patience in my heart.

Instead of rushing and raising my voice, I wake my child with a gentle hug. Breakfast and getting ready isn't just a routine, but a chance for little chats and laughs. I keep this calm, loving vibe all day, whether it's during homework, playtime, or mealtime.

Sure, spills happen and plans go sideways, but with visualization, I remember to meet those moments with a smile instead of a frown. Dinner and bedtime are our time to connect, share stories, and just enjoy being together.

If you're unsure about trying visualization, give it a shot. It's not about a perfect day, but about filling each moment with more understanding and love. It's amazing how a simple morning habit can make the whole day with your child more peaceful and joyful. Visualization isn't just a tool; it's a way to fill your parenting journey with more love and less yelling.

Hang In There

Parenting is a marathon, not a sprint. If we start off too fast, we'll soon find ourselves out of breath, unable to reach the finish line. Remember, we're not machines; we're beautifully imperfect humans, full of nuances and emotions. Especially when our children are little, the journey can feel relentless. Your little ones need you constantly, their demands are incessant, and there are moments when it feels like there's no space left to breathe. The tantrums hit, each one seemingly more challenging than the last, and it's all uncharted territory, especially if you're a first-time parent.

Take a moment to acknowledge these raw, real aspects of parenting. Try to recognize that it's okay to feel overwhelmed, or not to have all the answers. Accept this gentle reminder to slow down, to savor the small moments, even amidst the chaos, because the truth is, as our children grow, so do their worlds, and there will come a day when they don't need us quite as much. Many parents look back and wish they had savored those demanding early years a bit more, not rushed through them.

In our journey together, let's embrace our humanity, accept our flaws, and forgive ourselves for the bumps along the way. Cherishing each moment is key, as every challenge offers a chance to connect, teach, and understand more deeply. It's about being fully present, not rushing from one achievement to the next but moving at our own pace, fully engaged in the growth and learning experiences shared with our children.

Don't Worry about Tomorrow

As parents, it's like we have a built-in crystal ball. We catch our kids dodging homework or avoiding chores, and instantly, our minds jump years ahead: "Is this a sneak peek of their future? How will they ever cope with life's real challenges?" It's easy to get caught up in these whirlwind thoughts, to let them spiral into a storm of worry and self-doubt.

But here's a secret. Big worries often come from "thinking errors," exaggerated thoughts that don't really match up with reality. One of the sneakiest ones is catastrophizing. That's when we imagine the worst, even when it's far from likely. Our minds can be like a melodrama, always ready to turn a small scene into a full-blown production.

So, what's the better script? Live in the present. Right here, right now, is where you can really make a splash. The future is a journey your child will embark on, armed with the love and wisdom you're sharing today. So, let's focus on creating those heartwarming, belly-laugh-filled moments. Yes, the daily parenting grind can feel like a bit much at times, but just think – one day, you'll be helping your once-little ones unpack their boxes in a college dorm, wondering how those years zipped by so fast.

CONCLUSION

As we close the pages of *No Yelling Parenting Toolbox*, it's important to reflect on the heart of our journey together – the transformative power of the No-Yelling Formula. This journey, much like starting a weight loss diet, is not a quick fix but a meaningful shift towards a more peaceful way of communicating with our children.

Think about it: when you embark on a diet, you don't expect to shed weight in just 28 days, especially when old habits of eating and exercise are hard to break. Similarly, your default reactions to your child's misbehavior – those moments of frustration that bubble up into yelling – are obstacles in your path to calmer, more effective parenting.

But here's the hopeful truth: with intentionality and dedication, progress is not just possible, it's inevitable. The No-Yelling Formula isn't about never feeling frustrated or overwhelmed; it's about recognizing those feelings and choosing a different response. It's about breaking the cycle of reaction and regret and building a new habit of patience and understanding.

This transformation won't happen overnight. Just as changing your diet requires you to consciously choose healthier foods and more activity, changing your communication style requires a conscious commitment to pause, breathe, and respond calmly, even in the heat of the moment.

Your "default" reactions – those immediate, often regrettable responses – will challenge you. But remember, every effort you make towards speaking peacefully is a step towards a more harmonious home.

As you continue on this journey, be gentle with yourself. Celebrate your successes, learn from the setbacks, and keep moving forward. The No-Yelling Formula is more than just a tool for managing tantrums; it's a pathway to a deeper connection with your children, built on mutual respect and understanding.

So, as we part ways, carry with you the essence of the No Yelling Parenting Toolbox. Remember, change is a process, and progress, no matter how small, is still progress. Be intentional, be patient, and let the No-Yelling Formula guide you towards a future where every day is a little calmer, a little more understanding, and a lot more loving. Here's to the journey ahead – a journey of growth, learning, and, most importantly, love.

CUSTOMER REVIEW

Please Review My Book

I'm truly delighted that you read my book. I hope it has served as a valuable resource in your parenting journey. Your feedback is incredibly valuable and supports my mission to assist other parents.

Thank you for taking the time to leave a review—it truly means the world to me and I appreciate your help.

Carrie Khang

REFERENCES

American Academy of Pediatrics. (2015, November 21). Treating Children as Individuals. HealthyChildren.org. In Caring for Your School-Age Child: Ages 5 to 12. Retrieved from https://www.healthychildren.org/English/family-life/family-dynamics/Pages/Treating-Children-as-Individuals.aspx

Baby Wise Mom. (2020, May). How To Respond When Your Child has a Public Tantrum. Retrieved from https://www.babywisemom.com/logical-consequences-public-tantrums/

Belsky, G. (n.d). Why do kids misbehave? understood.org. Retrieved from https://www.understood.org/en/articles/why-do-kids-misbehave

Capriola, P. (2019, August 5). How Angry Parents Affect A Child: Tips for Raising Healthy Kids. strategiesforparents.com. Retrieved from https://strategiesforparents.com/angry-parents/

ChildLife Essentials. (n.d). 6 Ways To Decrease Mealtime Tantrums And Food Refusal. ChildLife Nutrition. Retrieved from https://childlifenutrition.com/6-ways-to-decrease-mealtime-tantrums-and-food-refusal/

Conway, S. (2021, June 13). Parenting Triggers: 3 important things you should know. mindfullittleminds.com. Retrieved from https://www.mindfullittleminds.com/managing-parenting-triggers/

Cross, J. (n.d). What Does Too Much Screen Time Do to Children's Brains? Health Matters. Retrieved from https://healthmatters.nyp.org/what-does-too-much-screen-time-do-to-childrens-brains/

Familydoctor.org Editorial Staff. (2022, August). Managing and Preventing Temper Tantrums. Reviewed by Peter Rippey, MD, CAQSM. familydoctor.org. Retrieved from https://familydoctor.org/managing-and-preventing-temper-tantrums/

Family Lives. (2018) Understanding and dealing with tantrums. Retrieved from https://www.familylives.org.uk/advice/toddler-preschool/behaviour/understanding-and-dealing-with-tantrums/

Bonnie Harris. (n.d). Don't take it personally. Retrieved from https://bonnieharris.com/dont-take-it-personally/

HealthMatters. (2020, July). Serious consequences of smartphone use by infants and toddlers. Retrieved from https://healthmatters.nyp.org/what-does-too-much-screen-time-do-to-childrens-brains/

Hwang, Eunhwa. (2020, July). Serious consequences of smartphone use by infants and toddlers. Retrieved from http://www.healtip.co.kr/news/articleView.html?idxno=3667

Debbie Pincus, MS LMHC (n.d). How to Get Control When Your Child Makes You Angry. Retrieved from https://www.empoweringparents.com/article/calm-parenting-get-control-child-making-angry/

Grogan, A. (2023, October). 5 Ways to Stop Mealtime Tantrums for Toddlers and Kids. Retrieved from https://yourkidstable.com/stop-mealtime-tantrums-and-enjoy-your-dinner/

Healthy Children Organization. (n.d). Treating Children as Individuals. Retrieved from https://www.healthychildren.org/English/family-life/family-dynamics/Pages/Treating-Children-as-Individuals.aspx

Health Matters (n.d). What Does Too Much Screen Time Do to Children's Brains? Retrieved from https://healthmatters.nyp.org/what-does-too-much-screen-time-do-to-childrens-brains/#:~:text=This%20research%20supports%20several%20previous,communication%20and%20problem%2Dsolving%20skills.

IncludeNYC (2021, October). The 5Rs of Consequences. Retrieved from https://includenyc.org/help-center/resources/the-5rs-of-consequences/

By Parenting Today Staff (2022, June). 7 Ways to Connect with Your Children. Retrieved from https://childdevelopmentinfo.com/family-building/7-ways-to-connect-with-your-children/

Um, Jeehae (n.d). Yelling is not parenting. Retrieved from https://ch.yes24.com/Article/View/31084

KidsHealth. (2015) Temper tantrums. Retrieved from https://kidshealth.org/en/parents/tantrums.html

TerryLevy (2018, March) Punishment vs Consequences. Retrieved from https://evergreenpsychotherapycenter.com/consequences-versus-punishment/

Lee, K. (2021, April). How to Set Healthy Boundaries for Kids. Retrieved from https://www.verywellfamily.com/whos-the-boss-how-to-set-healthy-boundaries-for-kids-3956403#:~:text=Lack%20of%20boundaries%20skews%20kids,seeds%20of%20narcissism%20and%20entitlement.

Lively, S. (2015, May 31). What You NEED to Know About Parenting Triggers. onetimethrough.com. Retrieved from https://onetimethrough.com/what-you-need-to-know-about-parenting-triggers/

López, M. A. (2022, December 27). 5 Misbehaviors in Children that We Shouldn't Allow. You are Mom. Retrieved from https://youaremom.com/parenting/learn-how-to-be-a-mom/behavior/misbehaviors-children/

Mayo Clinic Staff. (n.d).Infant and toddler health. Retrieved from https://www.mayoclinic.org/healthy-lifestyle/infant-and-toddler-health/in-depth/tantrum/art-20047845

Mayo Clinic Staff. (n.d).Temper tantrums in toddlers: How to keep the peace. Mayo Clinic. Retrieved from https://www.mayoclinic.org/healthy-lifestyle/infant-and-toddler-health/in-depth/tantrum/art-20047845

Michigan Alliance For Family. (n.d). Behavior is Communication. Retrieved from https://www.michiganallianceforfamilies.org/behavior-is-communication/#:~:text=Everybody%20communicates%20through%20behavior.,are%20not%20aware%20of%20it.

Morin, A. (n.d The importance of showing empathy to kids who learn and think differently. understood.org. Retrieved from https://www.understood.org/en/articles/the-importance-of-showing-empathy-to-kids-with-learning-and-thinking-differences

National Geographic Kids. (n.d). What is the right amount of screen time for kids? Retrieved from https://www.natgeokids.com/uk/parents/screen-time-for-kids/

NHS. (2016) Temper tantrums. Retrieved from: https://www.nhs.uk/conditions/pregnancy-and-baby/temper-tantrums/

Nichifiriuc, I. (n.d). Four Steps To A Peaceful Bedtime Routine. Retrieved from https://www.handinhandparenting.org/2018/07/peaceful-bedtime-routine-for-kids/

Norman, R. (n.d). Bedtime Battles: How To Avoid Stalling, Tantrums, & Constant Questions. amotherfarfromhome.com. Retrieved from https://amotherfarfromhome.com/bedtime-battles-toddlers-preschoolers/

Norman, R. (n.d). Common Habits That Help and Hurt Baby's Sleep: The Ultimate Guide. amotherfarfromhome.com. Retrieved from https://amotherfarfromhome.com/sleep-props/

OFS Healthcare. (n.d). Kids' screen time: How much is too much? Retrieved from https://www.osfhealthcare.org/blog/kids-screen-time-how-much-is-too-much/#:~:text=Yousuf%20said%20pediatricians%20generally%20recommend,per%20day%2C%20except%20for%20homework

Parenting Research. (2022, April). The Scientific Reason Why Yelling At Your Kids Doesn't Work. Retrieved from https://thoughtfulparent.com/scientific-reason-yelling-doesnt-work.html

Rogers K. (n.d). Screen time linked with developmental delays in toddlerhood, study finds. Retrieved from https://edition.cnn.com/2023/08/21/health/screen-time-child-development-delays-risks-wellness/index.html

Royal College of Psychiatrist. (2017) Dealing with tantrums: for parents, carers and anyone who works with young people. Retrieved from https://www.rcpsych.ac.uk/mental-health/parents-and-young-people/information-for-parents-and-carers/dealing-with-tantrums-for-parents-and-carers

Rymanowicz, K. (2015, March 30). Monkey see, monkey do: Model behavior in early childhood. Michigan State University Extension. Retrieved from https://www.canr.msu.edu/news/monkey_see_monkey_do_model_behavior_in_early_childhood

Shaikh, J. (2022, April). Why Is My Child Rude and Disrespectful? 6 Ways to Handle a Rude Child. Retrieved from https://www.medicinenet.com/why_is_my_child_rude_and_disrespectful/article.htm

Shealdon-Dean, H. (n.d). How to Set Limits on Screen Time. Retrieved from https://childmind.org/article/screen-time-during-the-coronavirus-crisis/

The Center for Parenting Education. (n.d). Coping With Sibling Rivalry. Retrieved from https://centerforparentingeducation.org/library-of-articles/sibling-rivalry/coping-sibling-rivalry/

The Center for Parenting Education. (n.d). How Do I Handle Sibling Rivalry? https://centerforparentingeducation.org/library-of-articles/top-10-tips/how-do-i-handle-sibling-rivalry/

The Understood Team. (n.d) The importance of showing empathy to kids who learn and think differently. Retrieved from https://www.understood.org/en/articles/the-importance-of-showing-empathy-to-kids-with-learning-and-thinking-differences

The Understood Team. (n.d) Through your child's eyes. understood.org. Retrieved from https://www.understood.org/articles/through-your-childs-eyes

Wiki How. (2021, August). How to Set Boundaries for Your Kids. Retrieved from https://www.wikihow.life/Set-Boundaries-for-Your-Kids

Wipfler,P. (n.d). Reaching For Your Angry Child.

Work Life Kids (2021, October 1). 5Rs: No-yelling formula for consequences. worklifekids.com. Retrieved from https://www.worklifekids.com/blog/2018/12/2/5rs-no-yelling-formula-for-consequences